This England's book of

Parlour Poetry

A Rhyming Reminder

of Half-Forgotten Verse

This England's Book of Parlour Poetry

©This England Books 1989
Second Edition 1991

Alma House, Rodney Road, Cheltenham,
Gloucestershire, GL50 1HT. Tel: 0242 577775.

Printed by
BPCC Wheatons Ltd.,
Marsh Barton, Exeter, Devon.

ISBN 0 906324 13 0 (Hardback)

This England

Contents

Preface 6
Give me a Ticket to Heaven 8
The Volunteer Organist 9
The Man Who Did It 10
The Indispensable Man 11
The Charge of the Light Brigade 12
Blind Bartimeus 14
St. Nicholas Day 15
Songs of Grace 16
The Reverie of Poor Susan 16
The Moss Rose .17
The Divine Office of the Kitchen 18
Problems of Etiquette for Animals 20
Pretty Polly Hopkins 21
The Star 22
Twinkle, Twinkle Little Star (Academic Version) . . . 23
An Overworked Elocutionist 24
Red Wing 25
The Tin Gee-Gee 26
Blanket Bay 28
The Beautiful Land of Nod 29
Buttercup Joe 30
Down the Vale 31
Kissing Cup's Race 33
Age 38
...and Middle Age 38
Let me Grow Lovely 39
...and wise 39
The Boy Stood on the Burning Deck 40
The Ballad of London River 42
The Beggar Man 43
Beatitudes for the Aged 44

(continued overleaf)

3

The Months 45
Lady Laburnum 46
A Garden Prayer 47
Garden Paradise 47
Going on an Errand 48
Solitude 50
Each In His Own Tongue 51
Distant Lands 52
Willow the King 53
Play up, and play the Game! 56
Drake's Drum 57
A Little Child Shall Lead Them 58
The Little Acorn 61
Speech 62
Myself 62
Thinking (or It's All in the State of Mind) 63
Miss Fogarty's Christmas Cake 64
The Lamplighter 65
The Sparrow's Song 66
A Christmas Gift 68
Only a Baby Small 69
Earwig Poem 70
Boats Sail on the Rivers 71
The Children's Hour 72
The Little Hero 74
My Mother 76
Somebody's Mother 78
The Touch of the Master's Hand 80
The Carpenter 81
The Pessimist 82
I'm Fine 83
Excelsior 84
Pilot 86
Flag of Britain 87
Good Night and Good Morning 88
Keeping His Word 90

Little Jim	92
Jim	94
The Sacrament of Peace	96
The Master is Coming	97
England's Sovereigns in Verse	101
...and a Short Version	103
The Upright Man	103
The Royal Prayer	104
The Prayer of the Tree	105
Child's Song in Spring	106
Old Grey Squirrel	107
My Creed	108
If	109
Curfew Must Not Ring Tonight	110
Life Unbroken	113
I Remember, I Remember	114
Voices of the Past	115
Table Rules for Little Folk	116
Refectory Grace	117
The Green Eye of the Little Yellow God	118
The Siege of Belgrade	120
Alliterations	121
Pronunciation for Foreigners	121
Christmas Day in the Workhouse	122
Which Shall It Be?	128
Lean Hard	130
Prayer for a Very New Angel	131
The Roman Centurion's Song	132
Norman and Saxon	134
Autumn Leaves	136
Grandmother's old Armchair	137
The Old Arm-Chair	139
The Perfect Guest	140
The Perfect Pest	140
Mother was a Lady	141
Alone on the Raft	142

Preface

by Roy Faiers, Editor of This England

Cold, cold it blows across the moor
The weary moor that I have passed . . .

S trange, isn't it, how odd lines of poetry come drifting back into your mind as you get older, sometimes from schooldays or even earlier. But how frustrating when you cannot fully recall all the words, or even find a book in the library with them in. I remember as a very small child climbing onto my father's knee to hear him recite, at my repeated request, the same piece of poetry over and over again. It contained the two lines quoted above and told the story of "a poor, half-frozen beggar man" who taps at a farmhouse door in the midst of winter seeking shelter from the biting blast. The farmer's children quickly bring the old man to the fireside and warm his stiffening fingers in their hands. Their kindness causes "a big round tear" to roll down the vagrant's wrinkled cheek . . .

That's all I could remember from childhood, but when a letter from a reader seeking the half-forgotten, half-remembered words of another old poem was published in our "Postbox" section in 1973, I added a postscript mentioning my poor old beggar man verse. Lo and behold, someone else in our vast army of readers knew it and sent the words in to me even though they had been written over a hundred years before! I then experienced that particular joy of being able to read again those treasured lines from long ago — not so much because of the quality of the poetry, but because of the memories they brought back of a happy childhood. I repeated the exercise for other readers and received an avalanche of answers and even more requests . . . that is how "Parlour Poetry" was born, and it has been a regular feature of *This England* ever since.

Over the years many hundreds of requests have been successfully answered, sometimes by scores of different readers living in various parts of the world. This in itself has brought untold delights to the seekers, but in a strange way those readers able to answer the queries have discovered a unique pleasure for themselves, that of helping to ease the frustration of others. As a result, many long-lasting pen friendships have been formed and they continue to blossom wherever English is spoken.

When possible, *This England* includes at least a snippet or two from the desired poem in the follow-up edition, but since space in the magazine is always at a premium we have often had to defer publication until such time as we could produce a book containing the bulk of them. This long-promised volume is the result. Needless to say, even though it contains more than 100 old favourites which many of you learned at school, or as in my case on a loving parent's lap, there are many dozens more awaiting publication . . . because "Parlour Poetry" is as healthy a feature of *This England* now as it ever was, and judging from the response to current requests it will go on tickling your poetic memories for many years to come.

Give me a Ticket to Heaven

Into a railway station crept a little child one night;
The last train was just leaving, and the bustle at its height.
The station-master standing there, looked down with wond'ring eyes
Upon this little maid — so frail in form, so small in size.
"Where is your father, little one? Are you alone?" he cried.
With tearful eyes she look'd up in his and thus replied:

> CHORUS:
> *"Give me a ticket to heaven,*
> *That's where Dad's gone, they say,*
> *He'll be so lonely without me,*
> *Travelling all that way,*
> *Mother died when I was born, sir,*
> *And left Dad and me all alone,*
> *So give me a ticket to heaven, please,*
> *Before the last train is gone."*

"My Daddy worked upon the line, but when I went to-night
To take his tea, he lay there on a shutter — oh! so white.
Then to a great big building his mates carried him away;
'He's booked for Heaven, poor old Dick!' I heard one of them say,
A station this must be — I thought to find the train I'd wait;
But finding none I ran on here — I hope I'm not too late."

8

The station-master said, "Come, little one I'll see you right.
A ticket to your father you shall have this very night."
He took her to the hospital; they let her see her Dad.
Though injured, he had not been killed, and oh! her heart was glad.
Then turning to that kind friend who had brought her all the way,
She said, "If I lose Dad again, I'll come to you and say —

CHORUS

The Volunteer Organist

The preacher in the village church one Sunday morning said
"Our organist is ill today, will someone play instead?"
An anxious look crept o'er the face of every person there
As eagerly they watched to see who'd fill the vacant chair.

A man then staggered down the aisle
    whose clothes were old and torn
How strange a drunkard seemed to me
    in church that Sunday morn
But when he touched the organ keys
    without a single word
The melody that followed
    was the sweetest ever heard.

Each eye shed tears within that church, the strongest man
    grew pale
The organist in melody had told his life's own tale
The sermon of the preacher was nothing to compare
With that of life's example who'd sat in the organ chair.

(continued overleaf)

9

And when the service ended, not a soul had left a seat
Except the poor old organist who started towards the street
Along the the aisle and out the door he slowly walked away
The preacher rose and softly said, "Good brethren let us pray."

The scene was one I'll ne'er forget as long as I may live
And just to see it o'er again all earthly wealth I'd give
The congregation all amazed, the preacher old and grey
The organ and the organist who volunteered to play.

The Man Who Did It

Somebody said it couldn't be done, but he with a
    chuckle replied
That "maybe it couldn't but he would be one who wouldn't say
    no till he'd tried."
So he buckled right in with a trace of a grin on his face.
    If he worried, he hid it.
He started to sing as he tackled the thing that couldn't be done.
    And he did it!
Somebody scoffed: "Oh, you'll never do that, at least, no one
    ever has done it."
But he took off his coat and took off his hat and the first thing he
    knew, he'd begun it!

With a tilt of his chin, and a bit of a grin, if any doubt rose
    he forbad it.
He started to sing as he tackled the thing that couldn't be done.
    And he did it!
There are thousands to tell you it cannot be done, there are
    thousands to prophesy failure;
There are thousands to point out to you, one by one, the dangers
    that wait to assail you.
But just buckle right in with a bit of a grin, then take off your coat
    and go to it.
Just start in to sing, as you tackle the thing that cannot be done,
    and you'll do it!

The Indispensable Man

Some time when you're feeling important
Some time when your ego's in bloom
Some time when you take it for granted
You're the best qualified man in the room
Some time when you feel that your going
Would leave an unfillable hole
Just follow these simple instructions
And see how it humbles your soul:
Take a bucket and fill it with water
Dip your hand in it up to your wrist
Pull it out, and the hole that's remaining
Is a measure of how much you'll be missed.
You may splash all you like when you enter
You may stir up the water galore
But stop and you'll find in a moment
That it looks quite the same as before.

The moral of this quaint example
Is to do just the best that you can
Be proud of yourself, but remember
There is no indispensable man!

The Charge of the Light Brigade

Half a league, half a league,
Half a league onward,
All in the valley of Death
Rode the six hundred.
"Forward the Light Brigade!
Charge for the guns!" he said:
Into the valley of Death
Rode the six hundred.

"Forward the Light Brigade!"
Was there a man dismay'd?
Not tho' the soldier knew
Some one had blunder'd:
Their's not to make reply,
Their's not to reason why,
Their's but to do and die:
Into the valley of Death
Rode the six hundred.

Cannon to right of them,
Cannon to left of them,
Cannon in front of them
Volley'd and thunder'd;
Storm'd at with shot and shell,
Boldly they rode and well,
Into the jaws of Death,
Into the mouth of Hell,
Rode the six hundred.

Flash'd all their sabres bare,
Flash'd as they turn'd in air,

Sabring the gunners there,
Charging an army, while
All the world wonder'd:
Plunged in the battery-smoke
Right thro' the line they broke;
Cossack and Russian
Reel'd from the sabre-stroke
Shatter'd and sunder'd.
Then they rode back, but not,
Not the six hundred.

Cannon to right of them,
Cannon to left of them,
Cannon behind them
Volley'd and thunder'd;
Storm'd at with shot and shell,
While horse and hero fell,
They that had fought so well
Came thro' the jaws of Death
Back from the mouth of Hell,
All that was left of them,
Left of six hundred.

When can their glory fade?
O the wild charge they made!
All the world wonder'd.
Honour the charge they made!
Honour the Light Brigade,
Noble six hundred!

ALFRED, LORD TENNYSON

Blind Bartimeus

Blind Bartimeus at the gates
Of Jericho in darkness waits:
He hears the crowd — he hears a breath
Say, "It is Christ of Nazareth!"
And calls in tones of agony,
"Jesus, have mercy now on me."

The thronging multitudes increase;
Blind Bartimeus, hold thy peace!
But still, above the noisy crowd,
The beggar's cry is shrill and loud.
Until they say, "He calleth thee!"
"Fear not; arise, He calleth thee!"

Then saith the Christ, as silent stands
The crowd, "What will thou at my hands?"
And he replies, "O give me light!
Rabbi, restore the blind man's sight."
And Jesus answers, "Go in peace
Thy faith from blindness gives release!"

Ye that have eyes yet cannot see,
In darkness and in misery,
Recall those mighty Voices Three,
"Jesus, have mercy now on me!"
"Fear not, arise, and go in peace!"
Thy faith from blindness gives release!"

HENRY WADSWORTH LONGFELLOW

St. Nicholas Day

St. Nicholas comes in the wild winter weather,
(Heigh ho! the frost and the snow);
Holly and mistletoe shining together,
Never a rose on the tree.

Children come hither, we're all merry making,
Gifts from St. Nicholas here for the taking,
Oh, what a welcome has he,
Oh, what a welcome has he!

CHORUS:
Oh, it's good to be gay on St. Nicholas Day,
So the folks say, merry and gay.
To sing at your work and to laugh at your play,
On St. Nicholas Day in the morning.

St. Nicholas comes with his fingers a-tingle,
(Heigh-ho! the sleet and the snow);
Hark to the sleigh-bells, how lightly they jingle,
Over the road from the sea.

He is the trav'ller who never grows weary,
He is the friend who is always so cheery,
Oh, what a welcome has he,
Oh, what a welcome has he!

HELEN TAYLOR

Many songs were written in praise of Grace Darling, the lighthouse-keeper's heroic daughter, who spent most of her short life on the wild and exposed North-eastern coast of England at Bamburgh. Here is one of them:

Songs of Grace

'Twas on the Longstone lighthouse
There dwelt an English maid
Pure as the air around her
Of danger ne'er afraid.
One morning just at daybreak
A storm-tossed wreck she spied
And tho' to try seemed madness
"I'll save the crew", she cried.

So she pulled away o'er the dashing spray
Over the waters blue,
"Help, help," she could hear the cry
Of the shipwrecked crew.
But Grace was an English maid
And a stalwart heart had she
So she pulled away o'er the dashing spray
And the crew she saved.

The Reverie of Poor Susan

At the corner of Wood Street, when daylight appears
Hangs a thrush that sings loud, it has sung for three years:
Poor Susan has passed by the spot, and has heard
In the silence of morning the song of the bird.

'Tis a note of enchantment; what ails her? She sees
A mountain ascending, a vision of trees;
Bright volumes of vapour through Lothbury glide,
And a river flows on through the vale of Cheapside.

Green pastures she views in the midst of the dale,
Down which she so often has tripped with her pail;
And a single small cottage, a nest like a dove's,
The one only dwelling on earth that she loves.

She looks, and her heart is in heaven: but they fade,
The mist and the river, the hill and the shade:
The stream will not flow and the hill will not rise,
And the colours have all passed away from her eyes!

WILLIAM WORDSWORTH

The Moss Rose

The Angel of the flowers one day,
Beneath a rose tree, sleeping, lay.
That spirit, — to whom charge is given,
To bathe young buds, in dews of heaven.
Awaking from his light repose,
The Angel whispered to the rose:
"For the sweet shade, thou givest me,
Ask what thou wilt. 'Tis granted thee".
"Then", said the rose, with deepened glow,
"On me, another grace bestow".
The spirit paused, in silent thought.
What grace was there, the flower had not?
'Twas but a moment, o'er the rose
A veil of moss the Angel throws.
And, robed in Nature's simplest weed,
Could there a flower, that rose exceed?

FRIEDRICH ADOLF KRUMMACHER

The Divine Office of the Kitchen

Lord of the pots and pipkins, since I have not time to be
A saint by doing lovely things and vigilling with Thee,
By watching in the twilight dawn, and storming
    Heaven's gates —
Make me a saint by getting meals and washing up the plates!

Lord of the pots and pipkins, please, I offer Thee for souls
The tiresomeness of tea-leaves, and the sticky porridge bowls!
Remind me of the things I need, not just to save the stairs,
But so that I may perfectly lay tables into prayers.

Accept my roughened hands because I made them so for Thee!
Pretend my dishmop is a bow, which heavenly harmony
Makes on a fiddle-frying pan: it is so hard to clean,
And ah, so horrid! Hear, dear Lord, the music that I mean!

Although I must have Martha hands I have a Mary mind;
And when I black the boots, I try Thy sandals, Lord, to find.
I think of how they trod our earth, what time I scrub the floor.
Accept this meditation when I haven't time for more!

Vespers and Compline come to pass by washing supper things.
And mostly I am very tired; and all the heart that sings
About the morning's work, is gone, before me into bed,
Lend me, dear Lord, Thy Tireless Heart, to work in me instead.

My Matins are said over night to praise and bless Thy Name
Before hand for to-morrow's work, which will be just the same:
So that it seems I go to bed still in my working dress —
Lord, make Thy Cinderella soon a heavenly princess!

Warm all the kitchen with thy Love, and light it with Thy Peace!
Forgive the worrying, and make the grumbling words to cease.
Lord Who laid breakfast on the shore, forgive the world which saith
"Can any good thing come to God out of poor Nazareth?"

CECILY HALLACK

Problems of Etiquette for Animals

Should a cassowary curtesy to a camel?
Should a porpoise say "Good morning" to a shark?
Should a salamander bow to a solitary cow
If he meets her in the village after dark?

Should barnacles wear billycocks or bowlers?
Should centipedes wear Wellingtons, or what?
If a lobster's out to tea and he's got a cold should he
Be allowed to keep his muffler on or not?

Should rhinoceroses bathe in public places?
Is a porcupine at parties quite the thing?
If a llama comes to call and he hasn't washed at all
Does it matter if one doesn't hear him ring?

Should a dolphin dilly-dally with a dog-fish?
Should a caterpillar parley with a snail?
If a guinea-pig should talk with a squirrel as they walk
Should the squirrel raise the topic of a tail?

Should a buffalo go golfing with a bison?
Should pelicans wear puttees on parade?
Should an eel wear evening dress when it causes him distress
While his tailor's bill is waiting to be paid?

Should hyenas laugh at things that are not funny,
Say, an antelope eloping with an elk?
Should storks go in for stilts and should grouse adopt the kilts?
May a winkle pull a cracker with a whelk.

ESME COOKE

Pretty Polly Hopkins

Oh! How do you do my Pretty Polly Hopkins
Oh! How do you do, How do you do.

Oh! None the better for seeing of you Mr. Tomkins
For seeing of you, For seeing of you.

Oh! Cruel, Cruel, Cruel Polly Hopkins
For telling me so, For telling me so.

If I should die my Pretty Polly Hopkins
Oh! Wouldn't you cry, Oh! wouldn't you cry.

I'd sob and cry, cry to be sure
To think you had not died long before, ore, ore.

Oh! Cruel, Cruel, Cruel Polly Hopkins,
To treat me so, To treat me so.

21

The Star

Twinkle, twinkle, little star,
How I wonder what you are!
Up above the world, so high,
Like a diamond in the sky.

When the blazing sun is gone,
When he nothing shines upon,
Then you show your little light,
Twinkle, twinkle, all the night.

Then the traveller in the dark,
Thanks you for your tiny spark!
He could not see which way to go,
If you did not twinkle so.

In the dark blue sky you keep,
And often through my curtains peep,
For you never shut your eye
Till the sun is in the sky.

As your bright and tiny spark
Lights the traveller in the dark,
Though I know not what you are,
Twinkle, twinkle, little star.

JANE TAYLOR

22

Twinkle, Twinkle Little Star
(Academic version)

Scintillate, scintillate, globule vivific,
Fain would I fathom thy nature specific,
Loftily poised in ether capacious,
Closely resembling a gem carbonaceous.

When torrid Phoebus refuses his presence,
And ceases to lamp us with fierce incandescence,
Then you illuminate the regions supernal,
Scintillate, scintillate, semper nocturnal.

Then the victim of hospiceless peregrination
Gratefully hails your coruscation;
He could not determine his journey's direction
But for your bright scintillating reflection.

UNKNOWN

Also:

Twinkle, twinkle little star,
I don't wonder what you are;
You're the cooling down of gases
Forming into solid masses.

UNKNOWN

An Overworked Elocutionist

Once there was a little boy whose name was Robert Reese;
And every Friday afternoon he had to speak a piece.
So many poems thus he learned, that soon he had a store
Of recitations in his head and still kept learning more.

And now this is what happened: He was called upon one week
And totally forgot the piece he was about to speak.
His brain he cudgelled. Not a word remained within his head!
And so he spoke at random, and this is what he said:

"My beautiful, my beautiful, who standest proudly by,
It was the schooner Hesperus — the breaking waves dashed high!
Why is this Forum crowded? What means this stir in Rome?
Under a spreading chestnut tree, there is no place like home!

"When freedom for her mountain height cried,
    'Twinkle, little star,'
Shoot if you must this old gray head, King Henry of Navarre!
Roll on, thou deep and dark blue castled crag of Drachenfels,
My name is Norval, on the Grampian Hills, ring out, wild bells!

If you're waking, call me early, to be or not to be,
The curfew must not ring tonight! O, woodman, spare that tree!
Charge, Chester, charge! On, Stanley, on! and let who will be clever!
The boy stood on the burning deck, but I go on forever!"

His elocution was superb, his voice and gestures fine;
His schoolmates all applauded as he finished the last line.
"I see it doesn't matter," Robert thought, "what words I say,
So long as I declaim with oratorical display."

CAROLYN WELLS

Red Wing

There once lived an Indian maid,
A shy little prairie maid,
Who sang a lay, a love song gay,
As on the plain she'd while away the day;
She loved a warrior bold,
This shy little maid of old.
But brave and gay he rode one day
To battle far away.

CHORUS:
Now the moon shines tonight on pretty Red Wing,
The breeze is sighing, the night-birds crying,
Far afar 'neath his star her brave is sleeping,
While Red Wing's weeping her heart away.

She watched for him day and night,
She kept all the camp fires bright,
And under the sky, each night she would lie,
And dream about his coming by and by;
But when all the braves returned,
The heart of Red Wing yearned,
For far, far away, her warrior gay
Fell bravely in the fray.

CHORUS

THURLAND CHATTAWAY

The Tin Gee-Gee

I was strolling one day down the Lowther Arcade,
That place for children's toys,
Where you can purchase a dolly or a spade
For your good little girls and boys;
And as I passed a certain stall, said a little wee voice to me;
"Oh I am a colonel in a little cocked hat
And I ride upon a tin gee-gee."

Then I looked and a little tin soldier I saw
In his little cocked hat so fine,
He'd a little tin sword that shone in the light
As he led a glittering line
Of tin hussars whose sabres flashed in a manner a-la-military,
While that little tin soldier rode at their head
So proud on his tin gee-gee.

Now that little tin soldier he sobbed and he sighed,
So I patted his little tin head;
"What vexes your little tin soul?" said I,
And this is what he said:
"I've been on this stall a very long time,
And I'm marked one-and-nine as you see,
While just on the shelf above my head
Is a fellow marked two-and-three.

"Now he hasn't got a sword and he hasn't got a horse
And I'm quite as good as he,
So why mark me at one-and-nine
And him at two-and-three?
And there's a saucy little dolly girl over there
Who used to smile at me
But now that I'm only marked one-and-nine
She turns up her nose at me,
She turns up her little wax nose at me
And flirts with two-and-three.

"And O she's dressed in a beautiful dress,
It's a dress I do admire,
She has pearly blue eyes that open and shut
When worked inside by a wire.
And once on a time when folk had gone
She used to ogle at me
But now, 'cause I'm only marked one-and-nine
She turns up her nose at me
She turns up her little snub nose at me
And carries on with two-and-three".

"Cheer up my little tin man", said I,
"I'll see what I can do.
You're a fine little fellow and it is a shame
That she should so treat you".

(continued overleaf)

27

So I took down the label from the upper shelf
And I labelled him two-and-three,
And I marked the other chap one-and-nine,
Which was very, very wrong of me,
But I felt so sorry for that little tin man
As he rode on his tin gee-gee.

Then that little tin soldier puffed with pride
At being marked two-and-three
And that saucy little dolly girl smiled once more
For he'd risen in life, do you see?
And it's so in life for I'm in love
With a maiden of high degree
But I am only marked one-and-nine
And there's another chap, two-and-three
And a girl never looks at a one-and-nine
With a possible two-and-three.

FRED CAPE

Blanket Bay

There's a wonderful ship called the White Pillow Slip
It's sailing to Blanket Bay

CHORUS:

So all aboard for Blanket Bay
Don't come back 'till the break of day
Roll him round in his little white sheet
Till you can't see his little bare feet
Then you tuck him up in his truckle bed
Hey high, oh little sleepy head.
Bless Mummy and Daddy and sail away
All aboard for Blanket Bay!

ANON

The Beautiful Land of Nod

Come cuddle your head on my shoulder dear
Your head like the golden rod
And we will go sailing away from here
To the beautiful Land of Nod.
Away from life's hurry and flurry and worry
And from earth's shadows and gloom
To a world of fair weather we'll float off together
Where roses are always in bloom.

Just shut up your eyes and fold your hands
Your hands like the leaves of a rose
And we will go sailing to those fair lands
That never an atlas shows.
On the North and the West they are bounded by rest
On the South and the East by dreams
'Tis the country ideal, where nothing is real
But everything only seems.

Just drop down the curtain of your dear eyes
Those eyes like a bright blue-bell
And we will sail out under starlit skies
To the land where the fairies dwell.
Down the river of sleep our barque shall sweep
Till it reaches that mystical isle
Which no man hath seen but where all have been
And there we will pause awhile
I will croon you a song as we float along
To that shore that is blessed of God
Then ho! for that fair land,
We're off for that rare land
That beautiful Land of Nod.

ELLA WHEELER WILCOX

Buttercup Joe

Now, I be a true bred country chap
Me Father comes from Fareham.
Me Mother she's got some more like I
And she well knows how to rear 'em.
Some people calls I 'bacon-fat'
And others 'turnip 'ead'
But I can prove I bain't no fool
Although I's country bred.

> CHORUS:
> *For I can drive a plough*
> *And milk a cow*
> *For I can rip or mow*
> *I'm as fresh as the daisies*
> *That grow in the field*
> *And they calls I Buttercup Joe.*

Now have yer seen my young woman?
They calls her Ower Mary
She works as busy as a bumble bee
Down in Sir John'es dairy.

And don't she make them dumplings nice
By gumph, I mean to try 'em!
And ask her 'ow she'd like to wed
A country chap like I am.

CHORUS

Some people they like haymaking
And others they like mowing
But the job of all that I like best
Is the job called turnip-hoeing.
I'll dust I up when I gets wed
To my old Mary Ann
I'll work for her and try me best
To please her all I can.

CHORUS

This is a Somerset dialect song, recorded in the Twenties by Albert (Laddie) Richardson, known as the Singing Sexton of Burwash in Sussex. He also recorded The Old Sow (Susanna's a funniful man) and sang on the wireless, although he was not a professional singer.

Down the Vale

When you come down the vale, lad,
   there's singing in the trees,
There's music in the gale, lad,
   and music in the breeze,
There's welcome and there's rapture,
   o'er moorland and o'er dale;
But none so glad as I am, lad,
   when you come down the vale.

Stars up above, find ye my love,
Tell him the the night is fair;
Peep from the skies into his eyes,
Leaving my image there.

(continued overleaf)

Where vale and coppice meet, lad,
    my tryst for thee I keep,
The harebells at my feet, lad,
    are smiling in their sleep;
And every bonny bird, lad,
    wings home his mate to greet,
And croons to me of love and thee,
    where vale and coppice meet.

Stars up above, find ye my love,
Tell him the night is fair;
Peep from the skies into his eyes,
Leaving my image there.

When we go down the vale, lad,
    the last, long Vale of Tears,
No terror shall prevail, lad,
    and there shall be no fears;
For though the shadows darken
    and every star be pale,
I shall not fear if you are near
    when we go down the Vale.

Angels above shall sing our love
In a divine refrain;
Where Love alone homage doth own,
Where Love alone doth reign!

GUNBY HADATH

Kissing Cup's Race

You've never seen Kissing Cup, — have you?
Stroll round to the paddock, my lord;
Just cast your eye over the mare, sir, —
You'll say that, upon your word,
You ne'er saw a grander-shaped 'un
In all the whole course of your life.
Have you heard the strange story about her,
How she won Lord Hillhoxton his wife?
No? Well, if you've got a few minutes,
I'll tell you why Kissing Cup, here,
Has lived in this lazy grandeur
Since the first time they let her appear
On a racecourse — to run for a wife, sir,
The loveliest girl in the land.
By Gad! 'twas a heart-thrilling moment
For them as stood on the Stand,
And knew the high stakes that were pending
On Kissing Cup's winning the race —
She ran for a woman's heart, sir, —
To save an old name from disgrace.

Here she is , sir; — now look her well over —
There isn't a fault to be found;
See her going — magnificent action!
You're right, sir; the mare is as sound
As she was on the day I rode her,
Just ten years ago last June:
I'll never forget how they cheered us,
The mare, and her jock, Bob Doon.

(continued overleaf)

He was always a reckless youngster,
My master, Hillhoxton, you know;
And when the old Marquis died, sir,
He seemed — somehow or other — to go
Right fair clean away to the devil;
And, being a fresh 'un, — you see? —
The "bookies" just fleeced him a good 'un —
I knew, sir, quite well how 'twould be;
I saw he would go down a mucker —
Be ruined, sir, sure as fate.
In his careless boyish folly
I saw that the fine old estate
Would be gambled away — the title
Be sullied, perchance, with shame.
I said to myself, "Bob Doon, boy!
You must save your old master's name."
He'd loved a quiet bit o' racing —
I'd been his head jock for years.
I remember the night he died, sir:
His bright eyes filling with tears,
He told me to mind the youngster,
To see that he didn't begin
To gamble — and always remembered
The Hillhoxtons rode to win.
He told me, above all, to see, sir,
That no scandal e'er touched the stud,
To be sure that our stables harbour'd
Nought but the purest blood.
He took my rough hand as he finished,
In the same old well-known grip,
As hundreds of times I'd seen him
A-grasping the ribbons and whip.

He didn't last very much longer —
I stood by the bed as he died,
And watched my old master's spirit
Start on its last long ride.

One night — I remember it well, sir, —
It must have been just nigh four years
After the old Marquis left us —
Very heavy at heart with fears,
I was sitting in one of the stables,
Not dreaming as no one was near,
A-thinking of how things were looking
A mighty sight too deuced queer.
I had turned round my head for a moment
To see as the nags were all right,
When I saw the young master a-standing
Behind me. I started! The sight
Of his face, pale and haggard,
Sent a rush of cold blood to my heart.
I knew, sir, that something had happened,
"Doon, Doon, my boy! why do you start?
Don't you know me?" he said. "Have I altered?
Have I changed so since yesterday?
No wonder, good God! I am ruined!
I've gambled the old home away.
But the worst — the poor girl, Lady Constance, —
You know how she loves me, old friend, —
What will she think of me now, Bob?
For pity's sake, Heaven defend
And keep her," he cried, "true as ever!
But no, no! I never can wed
You now. God bless you, my darling!
Forget me as if I were dead."
He wept like a child in his sorrow.
"Be a man! be a man, sir," said I;
"Trust to me, I can yet pull you through, sir, —
There's a mare in your stud that can fly.
I've kept her — I knew you were playing
Too fast, far too reckless, a game;
But there's Kissing Cup ready to run for
And save a Hillhoxton's name."

(continued overleaf)

When I saw that the lad was collected,
I asked him to turn and look
At the very first bet he had entered
On the very first page of his book.
He look'd at me — eyes full of wonder —
"That's three years! What d'ye mean?"
"My lord, you'll forgive me," I answered;
"Forgive me, I know you have been
Too hot, aye, too heedless by far, sir,
In your youthful and reckless career;
You've forgotten — just read for a moment
The words that you see written here."
I showed him the entry — five hundred
To one, clearly betted in "thous,"
Against the foal out of "Sweet Violet,"
By "Loving Cup," out of "Carouse."
"The foal, Kissing Cup, here, is ready
And fit, sir, to run for a life;
In the big race next week she will save you,
Will win you a fortune — and wife."
The boy couldn't speak for a moment.
His pallid lips moved in a groan;
Then he rallied, and grasping my hand, sir,
Held it just like a vice with his own.

The day of the race was a grand one,
But few knew the issue at stake;
We'd tried hard to keep it a secret
For the splendid old Marquis's sake.
As we cantered away past the stand, sir,
To give the "big swells" all a view,
Hardly one of 'em dreamt what 'twould mean, sir,
If the Hillhoxton "Chocolate and Blue"
Were beaten — none guessed that the girl there,
With her beautiful face, worn and thin,
Was murmuring a low prayer to Heaven
That her young lover's colours might win.

"All ready?" — a beautiful start, sir;
The line was as straight as could be;
"They're off!" the shout rang for a moment
Around us, and then seemed to me
As dying away in the distance,
While we scudded along the course
At a pace that was far too killing
To last: so I kept my horse
Well back in the rear to "the Corner."
Then I let the reins loose on her mane.
She passed through them all but just one, sir,
Lord Rattlington's colt, Sugar Cane.
Then I saw there would be a struggle:
I had known it for months long back,
That all as I need be afraid of
Was the old Baron's fast-flying "crack."
'Twas a terrible moment for me, sir:
The colt was three good lengths ahead.
I whispered a word to the mare, sir;
'Twas enough — she knew what I said.
Sweeping on down the hill like a rocket,
She got to the girths of the colt;
My heart gave a great throb of pleasure;
I made sure that he'd "shot his bolt."
But no! his jock hustled him up, sir;
His whip swishes fell like rain;
And the cry ran like fire up the course, sir.
"It's thousands on Sugar Cane"
The stand was reached, Sugar Cane leading.
Two seconds, and all would be o'er.
"Lord Rattlington wins!" No, not yet, though
We're neck sir, to neck — two strides more.
I saw in the great sea of faces
A girl's — pale, white as the dead —
I cried, "For God's sake, Kissing Cup, now!" —

'Twas over — we'd won by a head!

Age

Age is a quality of mind
If you have left your dreams behind
If hope is cold
If you no longer plan ahead
If your ambitions all are dead
Then you are old.

But if you make of life the best
And in your life you still have zest
If love you hold
No matter how the birthdays fly
You are not old.

ANON

. . . and Middle Age

Middle age has balance, it can sort out dross from gold,
It does not rush to catch things new and cast aside the old,
It is like a sun-washed harbour where ships of every size
Bring home from life's rough sailing, good bales of enterprise.

Middle age is crowded with multi-coloured things,
Though it means a little folding of youth's bright,
    strident wings
It means deep understanding which moulds instead of breaks
And helps to bind up ugly wounds of other folks' mistakes.

Middle age is gracious, it's steady and it's kind,
It has learned through hard experience to be a trifle blind
When youth shouts out its challenge and brandishes its torch
For one day youth will also come to rest within its porch.

Let me Grow Lovely

Let me grow lovely, growing old —
So many fine things do;
Laces, and ivory, and gold,
And silks need not be new;

And there is healing in old trees,
Old streets a glamour hold;
Why may not I, as well as these,
Grow lovely, growing old?

ANON

. . . and wise

Let me grow wiser, growing old
Like many old folk do
Who learn, as years grow on, to blend
The best of old with new —
Who learn to save their waning strength
For things the most worthwhile
To meet the jars and frets of life
With patience and a smile.

Who learn to view the years that stretch
Beyond the allotted span
As just the extension of a lease
Of usefulness to Man —
And from the lessons of the years
Life's meaning to unfold
Why may not I, as well as these
Grow wiser, growing old.

CLARA E. GRANT

The Boy Stood on the Burning Deck

The boy stood on the burning deck,
Whence all but he had fled;
The flame that lit the battle's wreck
Shone round him o'er the dead.

Yet beautiful and bright he stood,
As born to rule the storm;
A creature of heroic blood,
A proud, though childlike form.

The flames rolled on — he would not go
Without his father's word;
That father, faint in death below,
His voice no longer heard.

He called aloud — "Say, father, say
If yet my task is done!"
He knew not that the chieftain lay
Unconscious of his son.

"Speak, father!" once again he cried,
"If I may yet be gone!"
And but the booming shots replied,
And fast the flames rolled on.

Upon his brow he felt their breath,
And in his waving hair,
And looked from that lone post of death,
In still yet brave despair;

And shouted but once more aloud,
"My father, must I stay?"
While o'er him fast, through sail and shroud
The wreathing fires made way.

They wrapt the ship in splendour wild,
They caught the flag on high,
And stream'd above the gallant child,
Like banners in the sky.

There came a burst of thunder sound —
The boy — oh! where was he?
Ask of the winds that far around
With fragments strewed the sea! —

With mast, and helm, and pennon fair,
That well had borne their part;
But the noblest thing which perished there
Was that young faithful heart.

FELICIA HEMANS

This famous piece of parlour poetry was based on an actual incident in the Battle of the Nile when Nelson and his fleet smashed the French navy in 1798. The boy in the story was the 13-year-old son of Louis de Casabianca, captain of the French flag-ship. He remained at his post, alone, as the ship burned and his father lay dying. The correct title of the poem is "Casabianca".

41

The Ballad of London River

From the Cotswolds, from the Chilterns,
   from your fountains and your springs,
Flow down, O London river, to the seagull's
   silver wings.
Isis or Ock or Thame, forget your olden
   name, and the lilies and the willows
And the weirs from which you came.

The stately towers and turrets
   are the children of a day.
You see them lift and vanish
   by your immemorial way.
The Saxon and the Dane, they dared
   your deeps in vain,
The Roman and the Norman, they are past
   but you remain.

Your watergate stands open, o'er your
   turbid tide's unrest,
To welcome home your children, from the
   East and from the West,
O'er every ocean hurled, till the tattered
   sails are furled,
In the avenue of the Empire, in the highway
   of the world.

Then swing us to the surges, with the
   hurricane to grope,
With iron ills to grapple, with crushing
   odds to cope,
One with your flood are we, blood of your
   blood we be,
Beating eternal measure still to the pulses
   of the sea.

MAY BYRON

The Beggar Man

Around the fire one wintry night
The farmer's rosy children sat
The faggot lent its blazing light,
And jokes went round and careless chat.

When, hark! a gentle hand they hear
Low tapping at the bolted door
And thus, to gain their willing ear,
A feeble voice was heard implore:

"Cold blows the blast across the moor;
The sleet drives hissing in the wind;
Yon toilsome mountain lies before,
A dreary, treeless waste behind.

"My eyes are weak and dim with age;
No road, no path, can I descry,
And these poor rags ill stand the rage
Of such a keen, inclement sky.

"So faint I am — these tottering feet
No more my palsied frame can bear;
My freezing heart forgets to beat,
And drifting snows my tomb prepare.

"Open your hospitable door,
And shield me from the biting blast;
Cold, cold it blows across the moor,
The weary moor that I have passed."

With hasty step the farmer ran,
And close beside the fire they place
The poor, half-frozen beggar man,
With shaking limbs and blue, pale face.

(continued overleaf)

The little children flocking came,
And chafed his stiff'ning hands in theirs;
And busily the good old dame
A comfortable mess prepares.

Their kindness cheered his drooping soul,
And slowly down his wrinkled cheek
A big round tear was seen to roll,
And told the thanks he could not speak.

The children, too, began to sigh,
And all their merry chat was o'er,
And yet they felt, they knew not why,
More glad than they had done before.

LUCY AIKIN

Beatitudes for the Aged

Blessed are they who understand
My faltering step and palsied hand.
Blessed are they who know my ears today
Must strain to catch the things they say.
Blessed are they who seem to know
My eyes are dim and wits are slow.
Blessed are they who look away
When coffee was spilt on the table today.
Blessed are they with a cheery smile
Who stop to chat for a little while.
Blessed are they who never say
"You've told that story twice today."
Blessed are they who know the way
To bring back memories of yesterday.
Blessed are they who make it known
I'm loved, respected, and not alone.
Blessed are they who ease the days
On my journey home in loving ways.

ANON

The Months

January brings the snow,
Makes our feet and fingers glow.

February brings the rain,
Thaws the frozen lake again.

March brings breezes loud and shrill,
Stirs the dancing daffodil.

April brings the primrose sweet,
Scatters daisies at our feet.

May brings flocks of pretty lambs,
Skipping by their fleecy dams.

June brings tulips, lilies, roses,
Fills the children's hands with posies.

Hot July brings cooling showers,
Apricots and gilly flowers.

August brings the sheaves of corn,
Then the harvest home is borne.

Warm September brings the fruit,
Sportsmen then begin to shoot.

Fresh October brings the pheasant,
Then to gather nuts is pleasant.

Dull November brings the blast,
Then the leaves are whirling fast.

Chill December brings the sleet,
Blazing fire and Christmas treat.

SARA COLERIDGE

Lady Laburnum

Laburnum's a lady, the lilac's her lover
She promised to meet him, she vowed to be there;
But first she must go for green gloves to her glover,
And next she must comb the gold curls of her hair.
And turn them all twisty so smooth on her fingers,
And hook her silk bodice and draw her skirt strait
So on at her window she lingers and lingers,
Laburnum's a lady who always is late.

The lilac's her lover, her lover is ready;
He's splendid in purple, fine linen and lace,
His kerchief is perfumed, he looks for his lady,
His lady still looks in the glass at her face.
He fumes and he frets in regret and amazement
She promised to meet him and here is the date;
He sees but a glimpse of gold curls at her casement!
Laburnum's a lady who always is late.

He waits in the sun till his purple is faded,
He waits in the wind till the perfume has died,
The ruffles are dusty, and lover is jaded,
E'er comes out Laburnum at length in her pride.
Her keys in her pocket, her curls long and shining,
She comes to the lover who droops at the gate,
With splendour half gone and with glory declining —
Laburnum's a lady who always is late.

So weep for the fate of them — Lilac, Laburnum,
Who decked themselves out for each other so fine,
Each hoping for praises that cannot now earn 'em
And lone in her beauty see Laburnum decline.
Her flounces shall fray and her curls shall grow shorter
Let's write on her tomb with a tear for her fate,
"She kept her lover waiting three days and a quarter,
Laburnum's a lady who always is late."

FFRIDA WOLFE

46

A Garden Prayer

The kiss of the sun for pardon,
The song of the birds for mirth,
One is nearer God's heart in a garden,
Than anywhere else on earth.
The dawn of the morn for glory,
The hush of the night for peace,
In the garden at eve, say the story,
God walks, and His smile brings release.

DOROTHY FRANCES GURNEY

Garden Paradise

I sat in a beautiful garden
Dreaming away the hours
Bathed in the golden sunlight
Charmed by the scent of flowers
Soothed by the drowsy humming
Of bees in their search for store
And I wondered in all Creation what
Mortal could wish for more.

Going on an Errand

A pound of tea at one and three,
And a pot of raspberry jam,
Two new-laid eggs, a dozen pegs,
And a pound of rashers of ham.

I'll say it over all the way,
And then I'm sure not to forget,
For if I chance to bring things wrong
My mother gets in such a pet.

A pound of tea at one and three,
And a pot of raspberry jam,
Two new-laid eggs, a dozen pegs,
And a pound of rashers of ham.

There in the hay the children play —
They're having such fine fun;
I'll go there too, that's what I'll do,
As soon as my errands are done.

A pound of tea at one and three,
A pot of — er new laid jam;
Two raspberry eggs with a dozen pegs,
And a pound of rashers of ham.

There's Teddy White flying his kite,
He thinks himself grand, I declare;
I'd like to try to make it fly up sky high.
Ever so much higher
Than the old church spire
And then — but there —

A pound of three at one and tea,
A pot of new-laid jam,
Two dozen eggs, some raspberry pegs,
And a pound of rashers of ham.

Now here's the shop, outside I'll stop,
And run my orders through again.
I haven't forgot — it's better not —
It shows I'm pretty quick, that's plain.

A pound of three at one and tea,
A dozen of raspberry ham,
A pot of eggs, with a dozen pegs,
And a rasher of new-laid jam.

ANON

49

Solitude

Laugh, and the world laughs with you;
Weep, and you weep alone,
For this sad old earth must borrow its mirth,
But has trouble enough of its own.
Sing, and the hills will answer;
Sigh, it is lost on the air,
The echoes bound to a joyful sound,
But shrink from voicing care.

Rejoice, and men will seek you;
Grieve, and they turn and go.
They want full measure of all your pleasure,
But they do not need your woe.
Be glad, and your friends are many;
Be sad, and you lose them all —
There are none to decline your nectar'd wine,
But alone you must drink life's gall.

Feast, and your halls are crowded;
Fast, and the world goes by.
Succeed and give, and it helps you live,
But no man can help you die.
There is room in the halls of pleasure
For a large and lordly train,
But one by one we must all file on
Through the narrow aisles of pain.

ELLA WHEELER WILCOX

This poem was one of the most popular items at concerts from the beginning of the
century and many thousands of people, including the troops in the First World War,
knew it by heart.

Each In His Own Tongue

A fire mist and a planet —
   A crystal and a cell, —
A jellyfish and a saurian,
   And caves where the cave men dwell;
Then a sense of law and beauty,
   And a face turned from the clod —
Some call it Evolution,
   And others call it God.

A haze on the far horizon,
   The infinite, tender sky,
The ripe, rich tint of the cornfields,
   And the wild geese sailing high;
And all over upland and lowland
   The charm of the goldenrod —
Some of us call it Autumn,
   And others call it God.

Like tides on a crescent sea beach,
   When the moon is new and thin,
Into our hearts high yearnings
   Come welling and surging in —
Come from the mystic ocean,
   Whose rim no foot has trod —
Some of us call it Longing,
   And others call it God.

A picket frozen on duty,
   A mother starved for her brood,
Socrates drinking the hemlock,
   And Jesus on the rood;
And millions who, humble and nameless,
   The straight, hard pathway plod —
Some call it Consecration,
   And others call it God.

WILLIAM HERBERT CARRUTH

Distant
Lands

Where is now the merry party
I remember long ago,
Seated round the Christmas fireside,
Brightened by its ruddy glow?
Or in summer's balmy evenings,
In the field upon the hay?
They are all dispersed and wandered,
Far away, far away.

Some have gone to lands far distant
And with strangers made their home;
Some upon the world of waters
All their lives are forced to roam;
Some have gone from us forever,
Longer here they might not stay;
They have reached a fairer region
Far away, far away.

There are still some few remaining
Who remind us of the past,
But they change, as all things change here,
Nothing in this world can last.
Years roll on and pass forever,
What is coming, who can say?
Ere this closes many may be
Far away, far away.

This next poem was published in a book entitled "Gaudeamus" — a selection of songs for schools and colleges, around 1910, although the verses are probably much older than that. For non-cricket experts the King is the bat, the Duke is the ball, the three courtiers are the stumps, the palaces are wickets, and the green baize tree is the cricket bag which holds everything.

Willow the King

Willow the King is a monarch grand
Three in a row his courtiers stand
Every day when the sun shines bright
The doors of his palace are painted white
And all the company bow their backs
To the King with the collar of cobbler's wax.
So ho! So ho! may the courtiers sing,
Honour and life to Willow the King!

Willow, King Willow, thy guard hold tight
Trouble is coming before the night
Hopping and galloping, short and strong
Comes the Leathery Duke along
And down the palaces tumble fast
When once the Leathery Duke gets past.
So ho! So ho! may the courtiers sing,
Honour and life to Willow the King!

"Who is this," King Willow he swore,
"Hops like that to a gentleman's door?
Who's afraid of a Duke like him?
Fiddlededee!, says the monarch slim.
"What do you say my courtiers three?"
And the courtiers all said, "Fiddlededee!"
So ho! So ho! may the courtiers sing,
Honour and life to Willow the King!

(continued overleaf)

Willow the King stepped forward bold
Three good feet from his castle hold
Willow the King stepped back so light
Skirmished gay to the left and right
But the Duke rushed by with a leap and a fling
"Bless my soul!" says Willow the King.
So ho! So ho! may the courtiers sing,
Honour and life to Willow the King!

Crash the palaces, sad to see,
Crash and tumble the courtiers three!
Each one lays in his fear and dread,
Down on the grass his respected head;
Each one kicks, as he downward goes,
Up in the air his respected toes.
So ho! So ho! may the courtiers sing,
Honour and life to Willow the King!

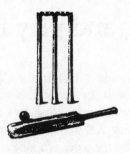

But the Leathery Duke he jumped so high,
Jumped till he almost touched the sky,
"A fig for King Willow", he boasting said,
"Carry this gentleman off to bed!"
So they carried him off with the courtiers three
And put him to bed in the green baize tree.
So ho! So ho! may the courtiers sing,
Honour and life to Willow the King!

"What of the Duke?", you may ask anon,
"Where has his Leathery Highness gone?"
O he is filled with air inside —
Either it's air, or else it's pride —
And he swells and swells as tight as a drum,
And they kick him about till Christmas come.
So ho! So ho! may his courtiers sing,
Honour and life to Willow the King!

E.E. BOWEN

Play up, and play the game!

There's a breathless hush in the Close to-night —
Ten to make and the match to win —
A bumping pitch and a blinding light,
An hour to play and the last man in.
And it's not for the sake of a ribboned coat,
Or the selfish hope of a season's fame,
But his Captain's hand on his shoulder smote —
"Play up! play up! and play the game!"

The sand of the desert is sodden red —
Red with the wreck of a square that broke;
The Gatling's jammed and the Colonel dead,
And the regiment blind with dust and smoke.
The river of death has brimmed his banks,
And England's far, and Honour a name,
But the voice of a schoolboy rallies the ranks:
"Play up! play up! and play the game!"

This is the word that year by year,
While in her place the School is set,
Every one of her sons must hear,
And none that hears it dare forget.
This they all with a joyful mind
Bear through life like a torch in flame,
And falling fling to the host behind —
"Play up! play up! and play the game!"

HENRY NEWBOLT

Sir Henry Newbolt (1862-1938) lawyer, poet and man of letters wrote this well-known and much-loved verse under the title *Vitai Lampada*. He was often called "the Navy's Kipling" because of the seafaring themes in many of his poems, most of which had a strong patriotic flavour. Another of his famous poems is *Drake's Drum* which follows . . .

Drake's Drum

Drake he's in his hammock an' a thousand mile away,
(Capten, art tha sleepin' there below?)
Slung atween the round-shot in Nombre Dios Bay,
An' dreamin' arl the time o' Plymouth Hoe.
Yarnder lumes the Island, yarnder lie the ships,
Wi' sailor lads a-dancin' heel-an'-toe,
An' the shore-lights flashin', an' the night-tide dashin',
He sees et arl so plainly as he saw et long ago.

Drake he was a Devon man, an' ruled the Devon seas,
(Capten, art tha sleepin' there below?)
Rovin' tho' his death fell, he went wi' heart at ease,
An' dreamin' arl the time o' Plymouth Hoe
"Take my drum to England, hang et by the shore,
Strike et when your powder's runnin' low;
If the Dons sight Devon, I'll quit the port o' Heaven,
An' drum them up the Channel as we drummed them
     long ago."

Drake he's in his hammock till the great Armadas come,
(Capten, art tha sleepin' there below?)
Slung atween the round-shot, listenin' for the drum,
An' dreamin' arl the time o' Plymouth Hoe.
Call him on the deep sea, call him up the Sound,
Call him when ye sail to meet the foe;
Where the old trade's plyin' an' the old flag flyin'
They shall find him ware an' wakin', as they found him
     long ago!

HENRY NEWBOLT

Sir Francis Drake is remembered not only as one of England's greatest sailors, and
the hero of the defeat of the Armada, but as the first Englishman to see the great
Pacific Ocean and to sail round the world.

A Little Child Shall Lead Them

The preacher was new to the circuit, youthful and full of zest,
And he entered the pulpit briskly, determined to do his best.
He had spent some hours on the sermon and viewed the
    result with pride;
It was sure to impress the officials sitting there at the side.
'Twas only a small village chapel set in the countryside deep,
Far from the noise and the bustle, mid green fields with
    cattle and sheep.

The chapel was filled to o'erflowing, with benches along
    the aisle,
The door to the vestry was open, and the children stood
    there awhile —
Till the opening hymn sung with gladness, by both the
    women and men,
Mingled harmoniously sweetly in Harvest Thanksgiving again.

And on this festival Sunday, the people had given with love —
The first-fruits, the best they could offer, in thanks to the
    Father above.
The tables in front of the pulpit were laden, as full as
    could be,
And the whole place looked liked a picture, decked in
    flowers and greenery.
Then the choir began singing softly, the organ a whisper
    of sound,
And the voice of a boy soprano soared in glory profound.

The children came in with their offerings, the big ones as
    well as the small,
Bringing their gifts to the Father, the Heavenly Giver of all,
Their faces so eager and smiling, placing their gifts with
    the rest,
Then taking their seats with the teachers, knowing
    they'd done their best.

One little maid seemed reluctant with her basket to part,
Till another child said, speaking clearly "You must give,
    with love in your heart —
For the sake of the Baby Jesus, who loves little children
    like you".
When with radiant smile she surrendered, "Oh yes, 'cause
    I love Him, too".

The preacher had watched fascinated, the children file
    slowly past,
Feeling humble and quite unworthy — And when there
    was silence at last,
Through the lump in his throat, and the tear-drops
    which fell all unchecked down his cheek,
He said, "Let us pray" and the people were still as he
    started to speak.

(continued overleaf)

The words from his lips came softly, but came from his
heart not his head,
And they all felt blessed and uplifted when his fervent
"Amen" was said.
The service proceeded to custom, till at last he stood up
to preach —
His splendid sermon forgotten, Twas their hearts not
their minds he must reach.

He spoke as much to the children who hung on his every word,
As to the grown-ups who listened, and nobody moved or stirred.
He told his story simply, how he, when a little child,
Was never taken to worship, but ran unforbidden and wild.

And laughed and jeered at his fellows who followed the
loving rule
Of their chapel-going parents and attended Sunday School.
And of a small crippled cousin, who came with her
parents to stay
And insisted one Sunday morning that "Johnny take me
to chapel today".

That too was a Harvest Thanksgiving, and the sullen
boy was amazed
At the spirit abroad in the chapel, and sat there silent
and dazed,
But avidly took in the story which the kindly preacher told,
Of the love which the tender Shepherd had for the
lambs of his fold.

"And my friends" the preacher concluded, "a little child
led me that day,
And now as my wife she still helps me, and is ever my
comfort and stay.
An eminent surgeon a miracle worked — through God
our Saviour and Friend,

And now she is well, and He's showered us with
　　blessings, never an end.
So the seed that was planted that Sunday fell not on
　　barren ground
And in learning of Him, and preaching His word, true
　　happiness I've found."

D.E.M. TRENBERTH

The Little Acorn

Long ago in changeful Autumn
When the leaves were turning brown,
From an oak tree's topmost branches
Fell a little acorn down.

And it tumbled by the pathway,
And a chance foot trod it deep
In the ground, where all the winter
In its shell it lay asleep.

With the white snow lying over,
And the frost to hold it fast
Till there came the mild spring weather
When it burst its shell at last.

First shot up a tiny sapling
Scarcely seen above the ground,
Then a mimic little oak tree,
Spread its tiny arms around.

Speech

Talk happiness. The world is sad enough
Without your woe. No path is wholly rough.
Look for the places that are smooth and clear,
And speak of them to rest the weary ear
Of Earth; so hurt by one continuous strain
Of mortal discontent and grief and pain.
Talk faith. The world is better off without
Your uttered ignorance and morbid doubt.
If you have faith in God, or man, or self,
Say so; if not, push back upon the shelf
Of silence all your thoughts till faith shall come.
No one will grieve because your lips are dumb.
Talk health. The dreary, never-ending tale
Of mortal maladies is worn and stale;
You cannot charm or interest or please
By harping on that minor chord disease.
Say you are well, or all is well with you,
And God shall hear your words and make them true.

ELLA WHEELER WILCOX

Myself

I have to live with myself, and so
I want to be fit for myself to know.
I want to be able, as days go by
Always to look myself straight in the eye.
I don't want to stand with the setting sun
And hate myself for the things I've done.

I don't want to keep on a closet shelf
A lot of secrets about myself
And fool myself, as I come and go
Into thinking that nobody else will know
The kind of man I really am.
I don't want to dress myself up in sham.

I want to go out with my head erect.
I want to deserve all men's respect
But here in the struggle for fame and pelf
I want to be able to like myself.
I don't want to look at myself and know
That I'm bluster and bluff and empty show.

I never can hide myself from me
I see what others may never see,
I know what others may never know
I never can fool myself, and so
Whatever happens I want to be
Self-respecting and conscience free.

EDGAR A. GUEST

Thinking
(or It's All in the State of Mind)

If you think you are beaten, you are
If you think you dare not, you don't
If you'd like to win, but think you can't
It's almost certain you won't.
If you think you'll lose, you've lost,
For out in the world you find
Success begins with a fellow's will
It's all in the state of mind.

Full many a race is lost
'Ere ever a step is run
And many a coward fails
'Ere ever his work's begun.
Think big and your deeds will grow
Think small and you'll fall behind
Think that you can and you will
It's all in the state of mind.   *(continued overleaf)*

If you think you're outclassed, you are
You've got to think high to rise
You've got to be sure of yourself before
You can ever win a prize.
Life's battles don't always go
To the stronger or faster man
But soon or late the man who wins
Is the fellow who *thinks* he can.

WALTER D. WINTLE

Miss Fogarty's Christmas Cake

As I sat by my window one evening, the letter man brought
unto me
A little gilt-edged invitation, "Gilhooley come over for tea."
I knew that the Fogartys sent it, and so I went just for old
friendship's sake
And the first thing they gave me to tackle was a slice of Miss
Fogarty's cake.

Miss Mulligan wanted to taste it but really there wasn't no use
They worked at it over an hour, and they couldn't get none of
it loose.
So Kelly came in with a hatchet and Murphy came in with a saw
That cake was enough by the powers, to paralyse any man's jaw.

Miss Fogarty proud as a peacock kept smilin' and drinkin' away
Till she fell over Flanigan's brogans and spilled the home brew
of her tay
"Oh, Gilhooley", she cried, "you're not eating, try a little bit more
for my sake"
"No thanks, Miss Fogarty", says I, "but I'd like the receipt of
that cake."

Maloney was took with the colic, McNulty complained of
    his head
McFadden lay down on the sofa and swore that he wished he
    was dead.
Miss Daly fell down in hysterics and there she did wriggle
    and shake
While every man swore he was poisoned for eatin' Miss
    Fogarty's cake.

CHORUS: *(To be repeated after each verse)*

There were plums and prunes and cherries, citron and raisins
    and cinnamon too.
Nutmegs, cloves and berries — and the crust it was nailed on
    with glue.
There were caraway seeds in abundance, sure could build up a
    fine stomach-ache
It would kill a man twice, after eating a slice, of Miss Fogarty's
    Christmas cake.

ANON

The Lamplighter

My tea is nearly ready and the sun has left the sky;
It's time to take the window to see Leerie going by;
For every night at tea-time, and before you take your seat,
With lantern and with ladder he comes posting up the street.

Now Tom would be a driver, and Maria go to sea,
And my papa's a banker and as rich as he can be;
But I, when I am stronger and can choose what I'm to do,
O Leerie, I'll go round at night and light the lamps with you!

For we are very lucky, with a lamp before the door,
And Leerie stops to light it as he lights so many more;
And oh! before you hurry by with ladder and with light,
O Leerie, see a little child and nod to him to-night!

ROBERT LOUIS STEVENSON

The Sparrow's Song

I'm only a little sparrow,
A bird of low degree,
My life is of little value,
But there's One who cares for me.
He gave me coat of feathers,
It is very plain I know,
With never a speck of crimson,
For it was not made for show.

But it keeps me warm in winter,
And it shields me from the rain
Were it bordered with gold or purple,
Perhaps it would make me vain;
And now that the spring-time cometh,
I will build me a little nest,
With many a chirp of pleasure,
In the spot I like the best.

I have no barn or storehouse,
I neither sow nor reap,
God gives me a sparrow's portion,
But never a seed to keep;
If my meal is sometimes scanty,
Close picking makes it sweet,
I have always enough to feed me,
And life is more than meat.

I know there are many sparrows,
All over the world we are found,
But the Father in heaven knoweth,
When one of us falls to the ground;
Though small we are never forgotten,
Though weak we are never afraid,
For the Father in heaven keepeth
The life of the creatures He made.

I fly through the thickest forest,
I alight on many a spray,
I have no chart or compass,
But I never lose my way;
And I fold my wings at twilight,
Wherever I happen to be,
For the Father in heaven watcheth,
And no harm can come to me.

And a postscript to the above:

Said the Robin to the Sparrow:
I should really like to know,
Why these anxious human beings
Rush about and worry so.

Said the Sparrow to the Robin:
Friend, I think that it must be
That they have no Heavenly Father
Such as cares for you and me . . .

A Christmas Gift

A mother was watching, one Christmas night
Nursing her babe by the candle light
And she lifted her eyes in the gathering gloom
For the Christ-child stood in the lowly room.
"What shall I give to thy child", He said
Softly caressing the sleeper's head.
"Nay", said the mother, "Oh angel-guest
Give her whatever Thou deemest best".

"But what shall I give her", He spoke again
"Ask and thou shalt not ask in vain.
Shall I touch her brow that her eyes may shine
With beauty that men will call divine?
Shall I touch her lips that they may flow
With songs of the best that the world may know?"
"Nay", said the mother, "these will not stay
Songs are forgotten, and hair turns grey".

"Then what shall I give her, oh Mother mild?
Ask what thou wilt for thy little child",
And the mother lifted her eyes above
"Give her purity, truth and love"
And the Christ-child turned to her, soft and mild
"Thou has chosen the best for thy little child
Be not afraid, though life be sore.
I will be with her for ever more".

Only a Baby Small

Only a baby small,
Dropped from the skies;
Only a laughing face,
Two sunny eyes.

Only two cherry lips,
One chubby nose;
Only two little hands,
Ten little toes.

Only a golden head,
Curly and soft;
Only a tongue that wags
Loudly and oft.

Only a little brain,
Empty of thought;
Only a little heart,
Troubled with naught.

Only a tender flower
Sent us to rear;
Only a life to love
While we are here.

Only a baby small,
Never at rest;
Small, but how dear to us,
God knoweth best.

MATTHIAS BARR

Earwig Poem

How odd it is that our papas
Keep taking us to cinemas
But still expect the same old scares
The tiger-cats, the woolly bears,
The lions on the nursery stairs
    To frighten as of old.
Consid'ring everybody knows
A girl can throttle one of those,
While choking with the other hand
The captain of the robber band,
    They leave one pretty cold.
The lion has no status now.
One has one's terrors, I'll allow,
The centipede, perhaps the cow,
    But nothing in the zoo,
The things that wriggle, jump or crawl,
The things that climb about the wall,
And I know what is worst of all —
    It is the EARWIG — ugh!
The earwig's face is far from kind:
He must have got a nasty mind:
The pincers that he wears behind
    Are poisonous, of course,
And Nanny knew a dreadful one
Which bit a gentleman for fun
    And terrified a horse.
He is extremely swift and slim
And if you try to tread on him
    He scuttles up the path;
He loves to burrow in your sponge,
And make one wild terrific plunge
    When you are in the bath;
Or else — and this is simply foul —
He gets into a nice hot tow'l
    And waits till you are dried,
And then when Nanny does your ears

He wriggles in and disappears
He stays in there for years and years,
	And crawls about inside,
At last, if you are still alive,
A lot of baby ones arrive,
	But probably you've died.
How inconvenient it must be!
There isn't any way, you see,
	To get him out again.
So when you want to frighten me
	Or really give me pain,
Please don't go on about that bear
And all those burglars on the stair,
I shouldn't turn a tiny hair
	At such Victorian stuff,
You only have to say instead
'THERE IS AN EARWIG IN YOUR BED,'
	And that will be enough.

A.P. HERBERT

Boats Sail on the Rivers

Boats sail on the rivers
And ships sail on the seas
But clouds that sail across the sky
Are prettier far than these.
There are bridges on the rivers,
As pretty as you please,
But the bow that bridges heaven
And overtops the trees
And builds a road from earth to sky
Is prettier far than these.

CHRISTINA ROSSETTI

The Children's Hour

Between the dark and the daylight
When the night is beginning to lower
Comes a pause in the day's occupation
That is known as the Children's Hour.

I hear in the chamber above me
The patter of little feet,
The sound of a door that is opened,
And voices soft and sweet.

From my study I see in the lamplight,
Descending the broad hall stair,
Grave Alice and laughing Allegra,
And Edith with golden hair.

A whisper and then a silence:
Yet I know by their merry eyes
They are plotting and planning together
To take me by surprise.

A sudden rush from the stairway,
A sudden raid from the hall!
By three doors left unguarded
They enter my castle wall!

They climb up into my turret
O'er the arms and back of my chair;
If I try to escape, they surround me;
They seem to be everywhere.

They almost devour me with kisses,
Their arms about me entwine,
Till I think of the Bishop of Bingen
In his Mouse-Tower on the Rhine!

Do you think, O blue-eyed banditti,
Because you have scaled the wall,
Such an old moustache as I am
Is not a match for you all!

I have you fast in my fortress,
And will not let you depart,
But put you down into the dungeon
In the round-tower of my heart.

And there will I keep you forever,
Yes, forever and a day,
Till the walls shall crumble to ruin,
And moulder in dust away!

HENRY WADSWORTH LONGFELLOW

The Little Hero

From Liverpool across the Atlantic, a big ship went sailing o'er
    the deep,
The skies bright with sunshine above us, the waters beneath
    us asleep.
Not a bad tempered mariner among us, a jollier crew
    never sailed.
'Cept the first mate a bit of a savage, but good seaman as ever
    was hailed.
One day he came up from below deck, a'grasping a lad by
    the arm,
A poor little ragged young urchin, who should have been home
    with his Marm.
Then the mate asked the lad pretty roughly, how he dared for to
    be stowed away,
A'cheating the owners and Captain, sailing, eating and all
    without pay.
Now the lad had a face bright and winning, and a pair of blue
    eyes like a girl's,
Looked up at the scowling first mate, and shook back his long
    shining curls.
Then he said in a voice clear and pretty, "My stepfather brought
    me aboard,

And he hid me away below deck, for to keep me he could not afford.

And he told me the big ship would take me, to Halifax town
      Oh! so far,

And he said "Now the Lord is your Father, Who lives where the
      good angels are".

"It's a lie" said the Mate, "Not your Father, but one of these big
      skulkers here,

Some milk headed, soft hearted sailor. Speak lad, tell the truth
      do you hear".

Then the mate took a watch from his pocket, just as if he was
      drawing a knife,

"If in ten minutes time you don't tell lad, here's the rope and
      goodbye to dear life".

Eight minutes went by in silence, says the mate then "Speak lad,
      say your say".

And his eyes slowly filling with teardrops, he falteringly said
      "May I pray".

An' the little lad kneels on the deck there, An' his hands he clasps
      o'er his breast,

As he must have done oft times at home lads, at night-time when
      going to rest.

And soft came the first words "Our Father" low and clear from
      those dear baby lips,

But low as they were, heard like trumpets, by every true man
      aboard that ship.

Every bit of that prayer he went through to "Forever, and
      Forever Amen,"

An' for all the bright gold of the Indies, I wouldn't ha' heard
      it again.

Off his feet was the lad sudden lifted, and clasped to the Mate's
      rugged breast,

And his husky voice whispered "God Bless You", As his lips to
      his forehead he pressed.

"You believe me now" then said the youngster. "Believe you", he
      kissed him once more,

"You'd have laid down your life for the truth lad, I believe you for
      now and ever more".

ANON

My Mother

Who fed me from her gentle breast,
And hushed me in her arms to rest,
And on my cheeks sweet kisses prest?
    My Mother.

When sleep forsook my open eye,
Who was it sung sweet hushabye,
And rocked me that I should not cry?
    My Mother.

Who sat and watched my infant head,
When sleeping on my cradle bed?
And tears of sweet affection shed?
    My Mother.

When pain and sickness made me cry,
Who gazed upon my heavy eye,
And wept for fear that I should die?
    My Mother.

Who dressed my doll in clothes so gay?
And taught me pretty how to play,
And minded all I had to say?
    My Mother.

Who ran to help me when I fell,
And would some pretty story tell,
Or kiss the place to make it well?
    My Mother.

Who taught my infant lips to pray,
And love God's holy book and day,
And walk in wisdom's pleasant way?
    My Mother.

And can I ever cease to be
Affectionate and kind to thee,
Who was so very kind to me,
   My Mother?

Ah, no! the thought I cannot bear,
And if God please my life to spare,
I hope I shall reward thy care,
   My Mother.

When thou art feeble, old and grey,
My healthy arm shall be thy stay,
And I will soothe thy pains away,
   My Mother.

And when I see thee hang thy head,
'Twill be my turn to watch *thy* bed,
And tears of sweet affection shed,
   My Mother.

For could Our Father in the skies,
Look down with pleased or loving eyes,
If ever I could dare despise
   My Mother?

ANN TAYLOR

Somebody's Mother

The woman was old, and ragged, and grey,
And bent with the chill of a winter's day;
The streets were white with a recent snow,
And the woman's feet with age were slow.

At the crowded crossing she waited long,
Jostled aside by the careless throng
Of human beings who passed her by,
Unheeding the glance of her anxious eye.

Down the street with laughter and shout,
Glad in the freedom of "school let out",
Came happy boys, like a flock of sheep,
Hailing the snow piled white and deep;
Past the woman, so old and grey,
Hastened the children on their way.

None offering a helping hand to her,
So weak and tired, afraid to stir,
Lest the carriage wheels or the horses' feet
Should trample her down in the slippery street.

At last came out of the merry troop
The gayest boy of all the group;
He paused beside her, and whispered low,
"I'll help you across, if you wish to go".

Her aged hand on his strong young arm
She placed, and so without hurt or harm,
He guided the trembling feet along,
Proud that his own were young and strong;
Then back again to his friends he went,
His young heart happy and well content.

"She's somebody's mother, boys, you know,
For all she's aged, and poor, and slow,
And someone, sometime, may lend a hand
To help *my* mother — you understand? —
If ever she's poor, and old, and grey,
And her own dear boy is far away."

"Somebody's Mother" bowed low her head,
In her home that night, and the prayer she said
Was: "God, be kind to that noble boy,
Who is somebody's son, and pride and joy."

Faint was the voice, and worn and weak,
But the Father hears when His children speak;
Angels caught the faltering word.
And "Somebody's Mother's" prayer was heard.

MARY DOW BRINE

79

The Touch of the Master's Hand

'Twas battered and scarred, and the auctioneer
Thought it scarcely worth his while
To waste much time on the old violin,
But held it up with a smile:
"What am I bidden, good folks," he cried,
"Who'll start the bidding for me?"
"A dollar, a dollar"; then, "Two!" "Only two?
Two dollars and who'll make it three?
Three dollars, once; three dollars, twice;
Going for three — " But no,
From the room, far back, a gray-haired man
Came forward and picked up the bow;
Then, wiping the dust from the old violin,
And tightening the loose strings,
He played a melody pure and sweet
As a carolling angel sings.

The music ceased, and the auctioneer,
With a voice that was quiet and low,
Said: "What am I bid for the old violin?"
And he held it up with the bow.
"A thousand dollars, and who'll make it two?
Two thousand! And who'll make it three?
Three thousand, once, three thousand, twice,
And going, and gone," said he.
The people cheered, but some of them cried,
"We do not quite understand
What changed its worth." Swift came the reply:
"The touch of a master's hand."

And many a man with life out of tune,
And battered and scarred with sin,
Is auctioned cheap to the thoughtless crowd,
Much like the old violin.
A "mess of pottage", a glass of wine;
A game — and he travels on.
He is "going" once, and "going" twice,
He's "going" and almost "gone".
But the Master comes, and the foolish crowd
Never can quite understand
The worth of a soul and the change that's wrought
By the touch of the Master's hand.

MYRA BROOKS WELCH

The Carpenter

No gaslight ever lit his shop;
He had no wheels to start and stop;
No hot, metallic engines there
Disturbed the shaving scented air;
His hands were engines, and his eye
His gauge to measure beauty by . . .
How gently time went by for him
Up in that workshop! which grew dim
At sunset time: and then he'd lay
His chisels down, and sweep away
The chips and shavings of the day;
But left upon the bench no less
Than that day's gain in comeliness;
Then shut the door, and slowly went
Under the rose to bed, content.

This poem appeared in the preface to "The Village Carpenter" by Walter Rose, but
no author or source was given.

The Pessimist

Nothing to do but work,
Nothing to eat but food,
Nothing to wear but clothes
To keep one from going nude.

Nothing to breathe but air,
Quick as a flash 'tis gone;
Nowhere to fall but off,
Nowhere to stand but on.

Nothing to comb but hair,
Nowhere to sleep but in bed,
Nothing to weep but tears,
Nothing to bury but dead.

Nothing to sing but songs,
Ah, well, alas! alack!
Nowhere to go but out,
Nowhere to come but back.

Nothing to see but sights,
Nothing to quench but thirst,
Nothing to have but what we've got;
Thus through life we are cursed.

Nothing to strike but a gait;
Everything moves that goes.
Nothing at all but common sense
Can ever withstand these woes.

BENJAMIN KING

I'm Fine

There's nothing whatever the matter with me,
I'm just as healthy as I can be.
I have arthritis in both my knees
And when I talk, it's with a wheeze.
My pulse is weak, my blood is thin,
But I'm awfully well for the shape I'm in.

I think my liver is out of whack
And a terrible pain is in my back.
My hearing's poor, my eyesight's dim,
Most everything seems to be out of trim.
My doctor says my days are few
For every week there's something new.

The way I stagger is just a crime,
I'm likely to drop at any time.
I jump like mad at the drop of a pin,
But I'm awfully well for the shape I'm in.

My teeth will eventually have to come out,
And my diet, I hate to think about.
I'm overweight and I can't get thin,
My appetite's such that it's bound to win,
But I'm awfully well for the shape I'm in.

Arch supports I have for my feet
Or I wouldn't be able to go on the street.
Sleep is denied me every night
And every morning I'm a sight.
My memory's failing, my head's in a spin,
But I'm awfully well for the shape I'm in.

The moral is, as this tale we unfold,
That for you and me who are growing old
It's better to say "I'm Fine" with a grin
Than to let them know the shape we're in.

ANON

Excelsior

The shades of night were falling fast,
As through an Alpine village passed
A youth, who bore, 'mid snow and ice,
A banner with the strange device,
Excelsior!

His brow was sad; his eye beneath
Flashed like a falchion from its sheath,
And like a silver clarion rung
The accents of that unknown tongue,
Excelsior!

In happy homes he saw the light
Of household fires gleam warm and bright;
Above, the spectral glaciers shone,
And from his lips escaped a groan,
Excelsior!

"Try not the Pass!" the old man said;
"Dark lowers the tempest overhead,
The roaring torrent is deep and wide!"
And loud that clarion voice replied,
    Excelsior!

"O stay," the maiden said, "and rest
Thy weary head upon this breast!"
A tear stood in his bright blue eye,
But still he answered, with a sigh.
    Excelsior!

"Beware the pine-tree's withered branch!
Beware the awful avalanche!"
This was the peasant's last Good-night;
A voice replied, far up the height,
    Excelsior!

At break of day, as heavenward
The pious monks of Saint Bernard
Uttered the oft-repeated prayer,
A voice cried through the startled air,
    Excelsior!

A traveller, by the faithful hound,
Half-buried in the snow was found,
Still grasping in his hands of ice
That banner with the strange device,
    Excelsior!

There in the twilight cold and grey,
Lifeless, but beautiful, he lay,
And from the sky, serene and far,
A voice fell, like a falling star,
    Excelsior!

HENRY WADSWORTH LONGFELLOW

Pilot

This was written 40 years ago by Leading Aircraftwoman Suzy Fletcher (now Mrs. Moss). She was stationed at Biggin Hill, Kent and the poem was published in the *RAF Journal*.

Have no fear for me when I fly by night
For I may wander freely with the stars
And taste of the wild intoxication of heaven.
Have no fear for me in the wind and the rain
For I am one with the sky and the racing clouds for ever.

I know that in an hour begrudged of time
My spirit, whirling through the skies,
May come to rest upon the edge of darkness;
But have no fear for me, for waking
I shall discover the brightness of eternity.

So in the beauty of the universe
Shall I take delight,
And in destruction and death and sorrow
Shall I find my freedom.

Flag of Britain

One of the many patriotic songs which used to be sung on Empire Day (24th May) by schoolchildren in all parts of the country, often round a flag-pole in the playground.

Flag of Britain proudly waving
Over many distant seas,
Flag of Britain boldly braving
Blinding fog and adverse breeze.
We salute thee and we pray
Bless, oh God, our land today.

Flag of Britain wheresoever
Thy bright colours are outspread,
Slavery must cease forever,
Light and freedom reign instead.
We salute thee and we pray
Bless, oh God, our land today.

Flag of Britain 'mid the nations,
May it ever speak of peace
And proclaim to farthest stations
All unworthy strife must cease.
We salute thee and we pray,
Bless, oh God, our land today.

But if duty sternly need it,
Freely let it be unfurled,
Winds of heaven they may speed it
To each quarter of the world.
We salute thee and we pray,
Bless, oh God, our land today. *(continued overleaf)*

Love of it across the waters,
Passing with electric thrill,
Binds our distant sons and daughters
Heart to heart with Britain still.
We salute it and we pray,
Bless, oh God, our land today.

Regions east and west united,
All our Empire knit in one
By right loyal hearts depended
Let it wave beneath the sun.
We salute it and we pray,
Bless, oh God, our land today.

ANON

Good-Night
and
Good-Morning

A fair little girl sat under a tree,
Sewing as long as her eyes could see;
Then smoothed her work and folded it right,
And said, "Dear work, good-night, good-night!"

Such a number of rooks came over her head,
Crying "Caw, caw!" on their way to bed;
She said, as she watched their curious flight,
"Little black things, good-night, good-night!"

The horses neighed, and the oxen lowed;
The sheep's "Bleat, bleat!" came over the road,
All seeming to say, with a quiet delight,
"Good little girl, good-night, good-night!"

She did not say to the sun "Good-night!"
Though she saw him there like a ball of light;
For she knew he had God's time to keep
All over the world, and never could sleep.

The tall, pink fox-glove bowed his head —
The violets curtsied, and went to bed;
And good little Lucy tied up her hair,
And said, on her knees, her favourite prayer.

And while on her pillow she softly lay,
She knew nothing more till again it was day,
And all things said to the beautiful sun,
"Good-morning, good-morning! our work is begun."

R. MONCKTON MILNES

Keeping His Word

"Only a penny a box," he said,
But the gentleman turned away his head
As if he shrank from the squalid sight
Of the boy who stood in the failing light.

"Oh sir," he stammered, "you cannot know",
And he brushed from his lashes a flake of snow
That a sudden tear might have a chance to fall,
"Or I think, I think you would take them all".

"Hungry and cold at our garret pane
Willie will watch till I come again
Bringing a loaf, the sun has set,
Not a crumb has he had for breakfast yet.

"One penny and then I can buy the bread",
The gentleman stopped. "And you?" he said.
"Oh I can put up with the hunger and cold
But Willie is only five years old.

"I promised our mother before she went,
She knew I would do it and died content,
I promised her, sir, through best, through worst,
I always would think of Willie first".

The gentleman paused at his open door,
Such tales he had often heard before,
But he felt in his purse in the twilight drear
"I've nothing less than a shilling here".

"Oh sir, if you'd only take the pack
I'd bring the change in a moment back,
Indeed you may trust me!" "Trust you, no!
Here is the shilling, take it and go".

The gentleman sat in his easy chair,
Around him his family gathered there,
He smiled on his children, and rose to see
The baby asleep on his mother's knee.

"And now, it is nine by the clock", he said,
"Time that my darlings were all in bed,
Kiss me goodnight, and each be sure
When you say your prayers to remember the poor".

Just then came a message, a boy at the door,
But 'ere it was uttered he stood on the floor,
Half breathless, bewildered, and ragged and strange,
"I'm Willie, Mike's brother, I've brought you the change.

"Mike's hurt, sir, 'twas dark, the snow made him blind,
And he didn't take notice a bus was behind
Till he slipped on the road and then it whizzed by,
He's at home in the garret, I think he will die.

"Yet nothing would please him, Sir, nothing would do,
But out through the snow I must hurry to you,
Of his hurt he was certain you wouldn't have heard,
And so you might think he had broken his word!"

When the garret they hastily entered, they saw
Two arms, mangled, shapeless, outstretched on the straw,
"You did it, dear Willie, God bless you", he said,
And the boy smiling gladly, sank back and was dead.

ANON

91

Little Jim

The cottage was a thatched one,
The outside old and mean,
Yet everything within that cot
Was wondrous neat and clean.

The night was dark and stormy,
The wind was howling wild;
A patient mother knelt beside
The death bed of her child.

A little worn-out creature —
His once bright eyes grown dim;
It was a collier's only child —
They called him Little Jim.

And, oh! to see the briny tears
Fast hurrying down her cheeks,
As she offer'd up a prayer in thought —
She was afraid to speak,

Lest she might waken one she loved
Far better than her life;
For there was all a mother's love
In that poor collier's wife.

With hands uplifted, see, she kneels
Beside the sufferer's bed;
And prays that He will spare her boy,
And take herself instead.

She gets her answer from the child,
Soft fell these words from him —
"Mother, the angels do so smile.
And beckon Little Jim.

"I have no pain, dear mother, now,
But oh! I am so dry;
Just moisten poor Jim's lips again,
And, mother, don't you cry."

With gentle, trembling haste she held
The tea-cup to his lips;
He smiled to thank her, as he took
Three tiny little sips.

"Tell father when he comes from work,
I said 'goodnight' to him;
And, mother, now I'll go to sleep," —
Alas, poor Little Jim.

She saw that he was dying —
The child she loved so dear
Had uttered the last words that she
Might ever hope to hear. *(continued overleaf)*

The cottage door was opened,
The collier's step is heard, —
The father and the mother meet,
Yet neither speak a word.

He knew that all was over,
He knew his child was dead;
He took the candle in his hand,
And walked towards the bed.

His quivering lips gave token
Of the grief he'd fain conceal,
And see, his wife has joined him —
The stricken couple kneel.

With hearts bowed down with sadness
They humbly ask of Him,
In heaven, once more to meet again,
Their own poor Little Jim.

EDWARD FARMER

Jim

There was a Boy whose name was Jim;
His Friends were very good to him.
They gave him Tea, and Cakes, and Jam.
And slices of delicious Ham,
And Chocolate with pink inside,
And little Tricycles to ride,
And read him Stories through and through,
And even took him to the Zoo —
But there it was the dreadful Fate
Befell him, which I now relate.

You know — at least you ought to know,
For I have often told you so —
That Children never are allowed
To leave their Nurses in a Crowd;
Now this was Jim's especial Foible,
He ran away when he was able,
And on this inauspicious day
He slipped his hand and ran away!

He hadn't gone a yard when — Bang!
With open Jaws, a Lion sprang,
And hungrily began to eat
The Boy: beginning at his feet.
Now, just imagine how it feels
When first your toes and then your heels,
And then by gradual degrees,
Your shins and ankles, calves and knees,
Are slowly eaten, bit by bit.
No wonder Jim detested it!
No wonder that he shouted "Hi!"

The Honest Keeper heard his cry,
Though very fat he almost ran
To help the little gentleman.
"Ponto!" he ordered as he came
(For Ponto was the Lion's name),
"Ponto!" he cried, with angry Frown,
"Let go, Sir! Down, Sir! Put it down!"
The Lion made a sudden stop,
He let the Dainty Morsel drop,
And slunk reluctant to his Cage,
Snarling with Disappointed Rage.
But when he bent him over Jim,
The Honest Keeper's Eyes were dim.
The Lion having reached his Head,
The Miserable Boy was dead!

When Nurse informed his Parents, they
Were more Concerned than I can say: —
His Mother, as she dried her eyes,
Said, "Well — it gives me no surprise,
He would not do as he was told!"
His Father, who was self-controlled,
Bade all the children round attend
To James's miserable end,
And always keep a-hold of Nurse
For fear of finding something worse.

HILAIRE BELLOC

The Sacrament of Peace

Thank God for sleep!
And, when you cannot sleep,
Still thank Him that you live
To lie awake.
And pray Him, of His grace,
When He sees fit, sweet sleep to give,
That you may rise, with new-born eyes,
To look once more into His shining face.

In sleep — limbs all loose-laxed and slipt the chains —
We draw sweet-close to Him from whom our breath
Has life. In His sole hands we leave the reins,
In fullest faith trust Him for life or death.

This sleep in life close kinsman is to death;
And, as from sleep we wake to greet the day,
So too, from death we shall with joy awake
To greet the glories of The Great Essay.

To His belov'd new life in sleep He gives,
And, unto all, awakening from sleep.
Each day is resurrection — a new birth
To nearer heaven and re-created earth —
To all Life's possibilities — of good
Or ill — with joys and woes endued —
Till that last, shortest sleep of all,
And that first great awakening from Life's thrall.

Thank God for sleep!
And when you cannot sleep,
Still thank Him for the grace
That lets you live
To feel the comfort of His soft embrace.

JOHN OXENHAM

The Master is Coming

They said, "The Master is coming,
To honour the town to-day,
And none can tell at whose house or home
The Master will choose to stay."
And I thought while my heart beat wildly
What if He should come to mine?
How would I strive to entertain
And honour the Guest Divine!

And straight I turned to toiling
To make my house more neat;
I swept and polished and garnished
And decked it with blossoms sweet.
I was troubled for fear the Master
Might come ere my task was done
And I hastened and worked the faster,
And watched the hurrying sun.

(continued overleaf)

97

But right in the midst of my duties
A woman came to my door:
She had come to tell me her sorrow,
And my comfort and help to implore.
But I said "I cannot listen
Nor help you any to-day;
I have greater things to attend to."
And the pleader went away.

And soon there came another —
A cripple, thin, pale and grey —
And said "O let me stop and rest
Awhile in your house I pray.
I have travelled far since morning,
I am hungry and faint and weak;
My heart is full of misery,
And comfort and help I seek."

But I said, "I am grieved and sorry,
But I cannot help you to-day.
I look for a great and noble guest"
And the cripple went away.
And the day wore on more swiftly
And my task was nearly done,
And a prayer was in my heart
That the Master to me might come.

And I thought I would spring to meet Him,
And serve Him with utmost care —
When a little child stood by me
With a face so sweet and fair —
Fair — but with marks of tear-drops,
And his clothing was tattered and old,
A finger was bruised and bleeding,
And his bare little feet were cold.

And I said, "I am sorry for you:
You are sorely in need of care,
But I cannot stop to give it —
You must hasten otherwhere".
And at these words a shadow
Swept o'er his blue-veined brow,
"Someone will feed and clothe you dear,
But I am too busy now".

At last the day was ended,
And my toil was over and done;
My house was swept and garnished
And I watched in the house alone —
Watched, but no footfall sounded
No-one paused at my gate,
No-one entered my cottage door,
I could only pray and wait.

I waited till night had deepened,
And the Master had not come:
"He has entered some other door" I said
"And gladdened some other home!"
My labour had been for nothing,
And I bowed my head and wept,
My heart was sore with longing
Yet in spite of it all — I slept.

Then the Master stood beside me,
And His face was grave and fair;
"Three times to-day I came to your door
And craved your pity and care:
Three times you sent me onward
Unhelped and uncomforted:
And the blessing you might have had was lost,
And your chance to serve has fled."

(continued overleaf)

"Oh Lord, dear Lord, forgive me!
How could I know it was Thee?"
My very soul was shamed and bowed
In the depths of humility.
And He said, "The sin is pardoned
But the blessing is lost to thee,
For comforting not the least of mine
You have failed to comfort Me.

"You are no worse than those who failed
Me in the days when first I came,
To that little town of Bethlehem
Where no-one knew My name.
Shepherds came from fields near by
To welcome this new king,
Wise men too from far away
Brought gold and myrrh for offering.

But for the rest the common men
Who failed to hear the angels cry,
They looked ashamed throughout my life
And questioned in perplexity:-
"Who is He in yonder stall
At whose feet the shepherds fall?"
Failed to hear the answer given:-
"Tis the Lord, the King of Glory."

This poem is also known as "Inasmuch" (from St. Matthew, XXV, v.45) and was
published by The Sunday School Union in "The Empire Reciter", probably as early
as 1880.

England's Sovereigns in Verse

Norman Kings

William the Conqueror long did reign;
William, his son, by an arrow was slain;
Henry the First was a scholar bright;
Stephen was king without any right.

Plantagenet

Henry the Second, Plantagenet's scion;
Richard the First was as brave as a lion;
John, though a tyrant, the Charter signed;
Henry the Third had a weakly mind.
Edward the First conquered Cambria dales;
Edward the Second was born Prince of Wales;
Edward the Third humbled France in its pride;
Richard the Second in prison died.

House of Lancaster

Henry the Fourth for himself took the crown;
Henry the Fifth pulled the French king down;
Henry the Sixth lost his father's gains.

(continued overleaf)

101

House of Tudor

Edward of York laid hold of the reins;
Edward the Fifth was killed with his brother;
Richard the Third soon made way for another.
Henry the Seventh was frugal of means;
Henry the Eighth had a great many queens.
Edward the Sixth reformation began;
Cruel Queen Mary prevented the plan.
Wise and profound were Elizabeth's aims.

Stuart Line

England and Scotland were joined by King James.
Charles found the people a cruel corrector;
Oliver Cromwell was called Lord Protector;
Charles the Second was hid in an oak,
James the Second took Popery's yoke.
William and Mary were offered the throne,
Anne succeeded and reigned alone.

Hanoverian Kings

George the First from Hanover came;
George the Second kept up the name;
George the Third was loved in the land,
George the Fourth was polite and grand;
William the Fourth had no heir of his own,
So Queen Victoria ascended the Throne.

When good Queen Victoria's long reign was o'er
Edward the Seventh the English crown wore;
George the Fifth rules the vast realm of England today
And "God Save the King!" all his subjects' hearts say.

UNKNOWN

And a Short Version:

Willy, Willy, Harry, Ste,
Harry, Dick, John, Harry Three
One, Two, Three Neds, Richard Two,
Henry Four, Five, Six, then who?
Edward Four, Five, Dick the Bad,
Harries Twain and Ned the Lad.
Mary, Bessie, James the Vain,
Charlie, Charlie, James Again.
William and Mary, Anna Gloria,
Four Georges, William and Victoria.

The Upright Man

The man of life upright, whose guiltless heart is free
From all dishonest deeds, and thoughts of vanity;
That man whose silent days in harmless joys are spent,
Whom hopes cannot delude, nor fortune discontent;
That man needs neither tower nor armour for defence,
Nor secret vaults to fly from thunder's violence.
He only can behold with unaffrighted eyes
The horrors of the deep and terrors of the skies.
Thus, scorning all the care that fate or fortune brings,
He makes the heaven his book, his wisdom heavenly things,
Good thoughts his only friends, his wealth a well-spent age,
The earth his sober inn — a quiet pilgrimage.

The authorship of this philosophical verse has been variously attributed to Sir Francis
Bacon (1561-1626) according to a manuscript in the British Museum, and to the poet
Thomas Campion (1567-1620) when it appeared in a song book published in 1601.

The Royal Prayer

This poem is thought to have been written by Queen Victoria's grand-daughter, Princess Marie Louise, shortly before she died in 1956. It came to light when it was found inside the cover of a diary belonging to a friend of the Princess, Mrs. Marguerite Manley, with the footnote: "Princess Marie Louise gave me this two weeks before she died". Mrs. Manley was well-known in London as a teacher of French, German and Hindustani, and the Princess herself had French lessons from her. Both lived to be 84 years old and became close friends.

Lord, help me to live from day to day
In such a self-forgetful way
That even when I kneel to pray
My prayers shall be — for others.
Help me in all the work I do
To ever be sincere and true
And know that all I'd do for you
Must needs be done — for others.
Let self be crucified and slain
And buried deep, and all in vain
May efforts be to rise again
Unless to live — for others.
And when my work on earth is done
And my time in Heaven's begun
May I forget the crown I've won
While thinking still — of others.
Others, Lord, yes others
Let that my motto be,
Help me to live for others
That I may live like Thee.

The Prayer of the Tree

You who pass by and would raise your hand
    against me, hearken ere you harm me,
I am the heat of your hearth on the cold
    winter night, the friendly shade screening
    you from summer sun,
And my fruits are refreshing draughts
    quenching your thirst as you journey on.
I am the beam that holds your house, the
    board of your table, the bed on which you
    lie, the timber that builds your boat.
I am the handle of your hoe, the door of your
    homestead, the wood of your cradle,
    the shell of your last resting place.
I am the gift of God and the friend of man.
You who pass by, listen to my prayer and
    Harm me not.

ANON

Child's Song
in Spring

The silver birch is a dainty lady,
She wears a satin gown;
The elm tree makes the old churchyard shady,
 She will not live in town.

The English oak is a sturdy fellow,
He gets his green coat late;
The willow is smart in a suit of yellow
While brown the beech trees wait.

Such a gay green gown God gives the larches —
As green as He is good!
The hazels hold up their arms for arches
When Spring rides through the wood.

The chestnut's proud, and the lilac's pretty,
The poplar's gentle and tall,
But the plane tree's kind to the poor dull city —
                I love him best of all!

                                    E. NESBIT

Old Grey Squirrel

A great while ago, there was a school-boy.
He lived in a cottage by the sea.
And the very first thing he could remember
Was the rigging of the schooners by the quay.

He could watch them, when he woke, from his window,
With the tall cranes hoisting out the freight.
And he used to think of shipping as a sea-cook,
And sailing to the Golden Gate.

For he used to buy the yellow penny dreadfuls,
And read them where he fished for conger-eels,
And listened to the lapping of the water,
The green and oily water round the keels.

There were trawlers with their shark-mouthed flat-fish,
And red nets hanging out to dry,
And the skate the skipper kept because he liked 'em,
And the landsmen never knew the fish to fry.

There were brigantines with timber out of Norroway,
Oozing with the syrups of the pine.
There were rusty dusty schooners out of Sunderland,
And ships of the Blue Cross line.

And to tumble down a hatch into the cabin
Was better than the best of broken rules;
For the smell of 'em was like a Christmas dinner,
And the feel of 'em was like a box of tools.

And, before he went to sleep in the evening,
The very last thing that he could see
Was the sailor-men a-dancing in the moonlight
By the capstan that stood upon the quay.

(continued overleaf)

He is perched upon a high stool in London.
The Golden Gate is very far away.
They caught him, and they caged him, like a squirrel.
He is totting up accounts, and going grey.

He will never, never, never sail to 'Frisco.
But the very last thing that he will see
Will be sailor-men a-dancing in the sunrise
By the capstan that stands upon the quay ...

To the tune of an old concertina,
By the capstan that stands upon the quay.

ALFRED NOYES

My Creed

I would be true, for there are those who trust me;
I would be pure, for there are those who care;
I would be strong, for there is much to suffer;
I would be brave, for there is much to dare.
I would be friend of all, the foe, the friendless,
I would be giving, and forget the gift;
I would be humble, for I know my weakness
I would look up — and laugh and love and lift.
I would be learning, day by day, the lessons
My heavenly Father gives me in his Word;
I would be quick to hear his lightest whisper,
And prompt and glad to do the things I've heard.

HOWARD ARNOLD WALTER

If

If you can keep your head when all about you
    Are losing theirs and blaming it on you,
If you can trust yourself when all men doubt you,
    But make allowance for their doubting too;
If you can wait and not be tired by waiting,
    Or being lied about, don't deal in lies,
Or being hated don't give way to hating,
    And yet don't look too good, nor talk too wise:

If you can dream — and not make dreams your master;
    If you can think — and not make thoughts your aim,
If you can meet with Triumph and Disaster
    And treat those two imposters just the same;
If you can bear to hear the truth you've spoken
    Twisted by knaves to make a trap for fools,
Or watch the things you gave your life to, broken,
    And stoop and build 'em up with worn-out tools:

If you can make one heap of all your winnings
    And risk it on one turn of pitch-and-toss,
And lose, and start again at your beginnings
    And never breathe a word about your loss;
If you can force your heart and nerve and sinew
    To serve your turn long after they are gone,
And so hold on when there is nothing in you
    Except the will which says to them: "Hold on!"

If you can talk with crowds and keep your virtue,
    Or walk with kings — nor lose the common touch,
If neither foes nor loving friends can hurt you,
    If all men count with you, but none too much;
If you can fill the unforgiving minute
    With sixty seconds' worth of distance run,
Yours is the Earth and everything that's in it,
    And — which is more — you'll be a man, my son!

RUDYARD KIPLING

Curfew Must Not Ring Tonight

Slowly England's sun was setting o'er the hilltops far away,
Filling all the land with beauty at the close of one sad day;
And the last rays kissed the forehead of a man and
　　maiden fair,
He with footsteps slow and weary, she with sunny floating hair;
He with bowed head, sad and thoughtful, she with lips all cold
　　and white,
Struggling to keep back the murmur, "Curfew must not
　　ring tonight!"

"Sexton," Bessie's white lips faltered, pointing to the
　　prison old,
With its turrets tall and gloomy, with its walls, dark, damp
　　and cold —
"I've a lover in the prison, doomed this very night to die
At the ringing of the curfew, and no earthly help is nigh.
Cromwell will not come till sunset"; and her face grew
　　strangely white
As she breathed the husky whisper, "Curfew must not
　　ring tonight!"

"Bessie," calmly spoke the sexton — and his accents pierced
　　her heart
Like the piercing of an arrow, like a deadly poisoned dart —
"Long, long years I've rung the curfew from that gloomy,
　　shadowed tower;
Every evening, just at sunset, it has told the twilight hour;
I have done my duty ever, tried to do it just and right —
Now I'm old I still must do it: Curfew, girl, must ring tonight!"

Wild her eyes and pale her features, stern and white her
    thoughtful brow,
And within her secret bosom Bessie made a solemn vow.
She had listened while the judges read, without a tear or sigh,
"At the ringing of the curfew, Basil Underwood must die."
And her breath came fast and faster, and her eyes grew large
    and bright,
As in an undertone she murmured, "Curfew must not
    ring tonight!"

With quick step she bounded forward, sprang within the old
    church door,
Left the old man threading slowly paths he'd often trod before;
Not one moment paused the maiden, but with eye and
    cheek aglow
Mounted up the gloomy tower, where the bell swung to and fro
As she climbed the dusty ladder, on which fell no ray of light,
Up and up, her white lips saying, "Curfew shall not ring
    tonight!"

She has reached the topmost ladder, o'er her hangs the great
    dark bell:
Awful is the gloom beneath her like the pathway down to hell;
Lo, the ponderous tongue is swinging. 'Tis the hour of
    curfew now,
And the sight has chilled her bosom, stopped her breath and
    paled her brow;
Shall she let it ring? No, never! Flash her eyes with
    sudden light,
And she springs and grasps it firmly: "Curfew shall not
    ring tonight!"

(continued overleaf)

Out she swung, far out; the city seemed a speck of light below;
She 'twixt heaven and earth suspended as the bell swung to
    and fro;
And the sexton at the bell rope, old and deaf, heard not the bell,
But he thought it still was ringing fair young Basil's
    funeral knell.
Still the maiden clung more firmly, and, with trembling lips
    and white,
Said, to hush her heart's wild beating, "Curfew shall not
    ring tonight!"

It was o'er; the bell ceased swaying, and the maiden stepped
    once more
Firmly on the dark old ladder, where for hundred years before
Human foot had not been planted; but the brave deed she had
    done
Should be told long ages after — often as the setting sun
Should illume the sky with beauty, aged sires, with heads
    of white,
Long should tell the little children, "Curfew did not ring
    that night!"

O'er the distant hills came Cromwell; Bessie sees him, and
    her brow,
Full of hope and full of gladness, has no anxious traces now.
At his feet she tells her story, shows her hands all bruised
    and torn;
And her face so sweet and pleading, yet with sorrow pale
    and worn,
Touched his heart with sudden pity — lit his eye with
    misty light;
"Go, your lover lives!" said Cromwell; "Curfew shall not
    ring tonight!"

ROSA HARTWICK THORPE

These words, written by Canon Scott Holland, who died in 1918, were read at the funeral of Policewoman Yvonne Fletcher, killed by Libyan terrorists outside their embassy in April 1984.

Life Unbroken

Death is nothing at all . . .
I have only slipped away into the next room.
I am I, and you are you . . .
Whatever we were to each other, that we are still.
Call me by my old familiar name,
Speak to me in the easy way which you always used.
Put no difference into your tone;
Wear no forced air of solemnity or sorrow.
Laugh as we always laughed at the little jokes we
        enjoyed together.
Play, smile, think of me, pray for me.
Let my name be ever the household word that it
        always was
Let it be spoken without effort, without the ghost of a
        shadow on it.
Life means all that it ever meant.
It is the same as it ever was;
There is absolutely unbroken continuity.
What is this death but a negligible accident?
Why should I be out of mind because I am out of sight?
I am waiting for you for an interval,
Somewhere very near, just around the corner.
All is well.

113

I Remember, I Remember

I remember, I remember
The house where I was born,
The little window where the sun
Came peeping in at morn:
He never came a wink too soon,
Nor brought too long a day, —
But now, I often wish the night
Had borne my breath away!

I remember, I remember
The roses, red and white,
The violets and the lily-cups —
Those flowers made of light!
The lilacs where the robin built,
And where my brother set
The laburnum on his birthday, —
The tree is living yet!

I remember, I remember
Where I was used to swing,
And thought the air must rush as fresh
To swallows on the wing:
My spirit flew in feathers then,
That is so heavy now, —
And summer pools could hardly cool
The fever on my brow!

I remember, I remember
The fir-trees dark and high;
I used to think their slender tops
Were close against the sky.
It was a childish ignorance,
But now 'tis little joy
To know I'm further off from Heaven
Than when I was a boy.

THOMAS HOOD

Voices of the Past

You wonder that my tears should flow
In listening to that simple strain;
That those unskilful sounds should fill
My soul with joy and pain —
How can you tell what thought it stirs
Within my heart again?

You wonder why that common phrase,
So all unmeaning to your ear,
Should stay me in my merriest mood,
And thrill my soul to hear —
How can you tell what ancient charm
Has made me hold it dear?

You marvel that I turn away
From all those flowers so fair and bright,
And gaze at this poor herb, till tears
Arise and dim my sight —
You cannot tell how every leaf
Breathes of a past delight.

You smile to see me turn and speak
With one whose converse you despise;
You do not see the dreams of old
That with his voice arise —
How can you tell what links have made
Him sacred in my eyes?

Oh, there are Voices of the Past,
Links of a broken chain,
Wings that can bear me back to times
Which cannot come again —
Yet God forbid that I should lose
The echoes that remain!

ADELAIDE ANN PROCTER

The last verse of this poem is carved into the back of the stairs at Willie Lott's Cottage at Flatford Mill, Suffolk.

Table Rules for Little Folk

In silence I must take my seat
And give God thanks for what I eat,
Must for my food in patience wait
Till I am asked to hand my plate.
I must not scold, nor whine, nor pout,
Nor move my chair, nor plate about.
With knife, or fork, or napkin ring,
I must not play, nor must I sing.
I must not speak a useless word,
For children must be seen, not heard.
I must not talk about my food,
Nor fret, if I don't think it good.
I must not say "the bread is old",
"The tea is hot" — "the coffee cold".
I must not cry for this, or that,
Nor murmur if my meat be fat.
My mouth with food I mustn't crowd,
Nor while I'm eating speak aloud.
Must turn my head to cough, or sneeze,
And when I ask, say "If you please",
The table cloth I must not spoil,
Nor with my food my fingers soil.
Must keep my seat when I have done,
Nor round the table sport, or run.
When told to rise, then I must put
My chair away with noiseless foot.
And lift my heart to God above
In praise for all His wondrous love.

Refectory Grace

Give me a good digestion, Lord,
And also something to digest;
But when and how that something comes
I leave to Thee, who knowest best.

Give me a healthy body, Lord;
Give me the sense to keep it so;
Also a heart that is not bored
Whatever work I have to do.

Give me a healthy mind, Good Lord,
That finds the good that dodges sight;
And, seeing sin, is not appalled,
But seeks a way to put it right.

Give me a point of view, Good Lord,
Let me know what it is, and why,
Don't let me worry overmuch
About the thing that's known as "I".

Give me a sense of humour, Lord,
Give me the power to see a joke,
To get some happiness from life,
And pass it on to other folk.

ANON

An ancient Prayer, found in Chester Cathedral.

The Green Eye of the Little Yellow God

There's a one-eyed yellow idol to the north of Khatmandu,
There's a little marble cross below the town;
There's a broken-hearted woman tends the grave of Mad Carew,
And the Yellow God forever gazes down.

He was known as "Mad Carew" by the subs at Khatmandu,
He was hotter than they felt inclined to tell;
But for all his foolish pranks, he was worshipped in the ranks,
And the Colonel's daughter smiled on him as well.

He had loved her all along, with a passion of the strong,
The fact that she loved him was plain to all.
She was nearly twenty-one and arrangements had begun
To celebrate her birthday with a ball.

He wrote to ask what present she would like from Mad Carew;
They met next day as he dismissed a squad;
And jestingly she told him then that nothing else would do
But the Green Eye of the Little Yellow God.

On the night before the dance, Mad Carew seemed in a trance,
And they chaffed him as they puffed at their cigars;
But for once he failed to smile, and he sat alone awhile,
Then went out into the night beneath the stars.

He returned before the dawn, with his shirt and tunic torn,
And a gash across his temple dripping red;
He was patched up right away, and he slept through all the day,
And the Colonel's daughter watched beside his bed.

He woke at last and asked if they could send his tunic through;
She brought it, and he thanked her with a nod;
He bade her search the pocket saying, "That's from Mad Carew",
And she found the little green eye of the god.

She upbraided poor Carew in the way that women do,
Though both her eyes were strangely hot and wet;
But she wouldn't take the stone and Mad Carew was left alone
With the jewel that he'd chanced his life to get.

When the ball was at its height, on that still and tropic night,
She thought of him and hastened to his room;
As she crossed the barrack square she could hear the
      dreamy air
Of a waltz tune softly stealing thro' the gloom.

His door was open wide, with silver moonlight shining
      through;
The place was wet and slipp'ry where she trod;
An ugly knife lay buried in the heart of Mad Carew,
'Twas the "Vengeance of the Little Yellow God".

There's a one-eyed yellow idol to the north of Khatmandu,
There's a little marble cross below the town;
There's a broken-hearted woman tends the grave of Mad Carew,
And the Yellow God forever gazes down.

J. MILTON HAYES

The Siege of Belgrade

A classic and probably unequalled example of "apt alliteration's artful aid"
— the only letter missing is "J".

An Austrian Army, awfully arrayed,
Boldly by battery besieged Belgrade.
Cossack commanders cannonading come,
Dealing destruction's devastating doom.
Every endeavour engineers essay,
For fame, for fortune fighting — furious fray!
Generals 'gainst generals grapple — gracious God!
How honours Heaven heroic hardihood!
Infuriate, indiscriminate in ill,
Kindred kill kinsmen, kinsmen kindred kill.
Labour low levels longest, loftiest lines;
Men march 'mid mounds, 'mid moles, 'mid murderous mines;
Now noxious, noisy numbers nothing, naught
Of outward obstacles, opposing ought;
Poor patriots, partly purchased, partly pressed,
Quite quaking, quickly "Quarter! Quarter!" quest,
Reason returns, religious right redounds,
Suwarrow stops such sanguinary sounds.
Truce to thee, Turkey! Triumph to thy train,
Unwise, unjust, unmerciful Ukraine!
Vanish, vain victory! vanish, victory vain!
Why wish we warfare? Wherefore welcome were
Xerxes, Ximenes, Xanthus, Xavier?
Yield, yield, ye youths! ye yeoman, yield your yell!
Zeus', Zarpater's, Zoroaster's zeal,
Attracting all, arms against acts appeal!

ALARIC ALEXANDER WATTS

120

Alliterations

Ten thousand trippers took twenty-three trains
To take them to Trincomalee.
They talked, they tittered then took their tea,
The tales they told together then!
The tricks they tried till ten to ten!
Till tardy time told them the tale
To take themselves to the townward trail.

Pronunciation for Foreigners

I take it you already know
Of tough and bough and cough and dough?
Others may stumble, but not you,
On hiccough, thorough, lough and through?
Well done! and now you wish perhaps
To learn of less familiar traps?

Beware of heard, a dreadful word,
That looks like beard and sounds like bird.
And dead: it's said like bed, not bead —
For goodness sake don't call it "deed"!
Watch out for meat and great and threat
(They rhyme with suite and straight and debt).

A moth is not a moth in mother
Nor both in bother, broth in brother.
And here is not a match for there,
Nor dear and fear for bear and pear,
And then there's dose and rose and lose —
Just look them up — and goose and choose,
And cork and work and card and ward.
And font and front and word and sword,
And do and go and thwart and cart —
Come, come, I've hardly made a start!
A dreadful language? Man alive,
I'd mastered it when I was five!

ANON

121

Christmas Day in the Workhouse

It is Christmas Day in the Workhouse,
And the cold bare walls are bright
With garlands of green and holly,
And the place is a pleasant sight:
For with clean-washed hands and faces,
In a long and hungry line
The paupers sit at the tables
For this is the hour they dine.

And the guardians and their ladies,
Although the wind is east,
Have come in their furs and wrappers,
To watch their charges feast;
To smile and be condescending,
Put pudding on pauper plates,
To be hosts at the workhouse banquet
They've paid for — with the rates.

Oh, the paupers are meek and lowly
With their "Thank'ee kindly, mum's"
So long as they fill their stomachs,
What matter it whence it comes?
But one of the old men mutters,
And pushes his plate aside:
"Great God!" he cries; "but it chokes me!
For this is the day *she* died."

The guardians gazed in horror,
The master's face went white;
"Did a pauper refuse the pudding?"
"Could their ears believe aright?"
Then the ladies clutched their husbands,
Thinking the man would die,
Struck by a bolt, or something,
By the outraged One on high.

But the pauper sat for a moment,
Then rose 'mid a silence grim,
For the others had ceased to chatter
And trembled in every limb.
He looked at the guardians' ladies,
Then, eyeing their lords, he said,
"I eat not the food of villains
Whose hands are foul and red:

"Whose victims cry for vengeance
From their dank, unhallowed graves."
"He's drunk!" said the workhouse master,
"Or else he's mad and raves."
"Not drunk or mad," cried the pauper,
"But only a hunted beast,
Who, torn by the hounds and mangled,
Declines the vulture's feast.

(continued overleaf)

"I care not a curse for the guardians,
And I won't be dragged away.
Just let me have the fit out,
It's only on Christmas Day
The black past comes to goad me,
And prey on my burning brain;
I'll tell you the rest in a whisper, —
I swear I won't shout again.

"Keep your hands off me, curse you!
Hear me right out to the end.
You come here to see how paupers
The season of Christmas spend.
You come here to watch us feeding,
As they watch the captured beast.
Hear why a penniless pauper
Spits on your paltry feast.

"Do you think I will take your bounty,
And let you smile and think
You're doing a noble action
With the parish's meat and drink?
Where is my wife, you traitors —
The poor old wife you slew?
Yes, by the God above us,
My Nance was killed by you!

"Last winter my wife lay dying,
Starved in a filthy den;
I had never been to the parish, —
I came to the parish then.
I swallowed my pride in coming,
For, ere the ruin came,
I held up my head as a trader,
And I bore a spotless name.

"I came to the parish, craving
Bread for a starving wife,
Bread for the woman who'd loved me
Through fifty years of life;
And what do you think they told me,
Mocking my awful grief?
That 'the House' was open to us,
But they wouldn't give 'out relief'.

"I slunk to the filthy alley —
'Twas a cold, raw Christmas eve —
And the bakers' shops were open,
Tempting a man to thieve;
But I clenched my fists together,
Holding my head awry,
So I came to her empty-handed
And mournfully told her why.

"Then I told her 'the House' was open;
She had heard of the ways of *that*,
For her bloodless cheeks went crimson,
And up in her rags she sat,
Crying, 'Bide the Christmas here, John,
We've never had one apart;
I think I can bear the hunger, —
The other would break my heart.'

(continued overleaf)

"All through that eve I watched her,
Holding her hand in mine,
Praying the Lord, and weeping,
Till my lips were salt as brine.
I asked her once if she hungered,
And as she answered 'No',
The moon shone in at the window
Set in a wreath of snow.

"Then the room was bathed in glory,
And I saw in my darling's eyes
The far-away look of wonder
That comes when the spirit flies;
And her lips were parched and parted,
And her reason came and went,
For she raved of our home in Devon,
Where our happiest years were spent.

"And the accents long forgotten,
Came back to the tongue once more,
For she talked like the country lassie
I woo'd by the Devon shore.
Then she rose to her feet and trembled,
And fell on the rags and moaned,
And, 'Give me a crust — I'm famished —
For the love of God!' she groaned.

"I rushed from the room like a madman,
And flew to the workhouse gate,
Crying, 'Food for a dying woman!'
And the answer came, 'Too late.'
They drove me away with curses;
Then I fought with a dog in the street,
And tore from the mongrel's clutches
A crust he was trying to eat.

"Back through the filthy by-lanes!
Back, through the trampled slush!
Up to the crazy garret,
Wrapped in an awful hush.
My heart sank down at the threshold,
And I paused with a sudden thrill,
For there in the silv'ry moonlight
My Nance lay, cold and still.

"Up to the blackened ceiling
The sunken eyes were cast —
I knew on those lips all bloodless
My name had been the last;
She'd called for her absent husband —
O God! had I but known! —
Had called in vain, and in anguish
Had died in that den — *alone.*

"Yes, there, in a land of plenty,
Lay a loving woman dead,
Cruelly starved and murdered
For a loaf of the parish bread.
At yonder gate, last Christmas,
I craved for a human life.
You, who would feast us paupers,
What of my murdered wife?

.   .   .   .   .   .

"There, get ye gone to your dinners;
Don't mind me in the least;
Think of the happy paupers
Eating your Christmas feast;
And when you recount their blessings
In your smug parochial way,
Say what you did for *her,* too,
Only last Christmas Day."

GEORGE R. SIMS

Which Shall It Be?

The author of this poem, who lived from 1827 to 1879, was a descendant of John Eliot, the "Apostle of the Indians," who first preached Christianity to the Red Indians, and first translated the Bible into their own tongue in 1663. The poem shows that John Eliot's loving spirit was still animating his descendants after 200 years.

"Which shall it be? Which shall it be?"
I looked at John — John looked at me;
(Dear, patient John, who loves me yet
As well as though my locks were jet);
And when I found that I must speak,
My voice seemed strangely low and weak:
"Tell me again what Robert said."
And then I, listening, bent my head.
"This is his letter: 'I will give
A house and land while you shall live,
If, in return, from out your seven,
One child to me for aye is given.' "
I looked at John's old garments worn,
I thought of all that John had borne
Of poverty and work and care,
Which I, though willing, could not share;
I thought of seven mouths to feed,
Of seven little children's need,
And then of this. "Come, John," said I,
"We'll choose among them as they lie
Asleep"; so, walking hand in hand,
Dear John and I surveyed our band.
First to the cradle lightly stepped,
Where the new nameless baby slept.
"Shall it be Baby?" whispered John.
I took his hand and hurried on
To Lily's crib. Her sleeping grasp
Held her old doll within its clasp;
Her dark curls lay like gold alight,
A glory 'gainst the pillow white.
Softly her father stooped to lay

His rough hand down in loving way,
When dream or whisper made her stir,
Then huskily said John, "Not her, not her!"
We stopped beside the trundle-bed,
And one long ray of lamplight shed
Athwart the boyish faces there,
In sleep so pitiful and fair;
I saw on Jamie's rough, red cheek
A tear undried. Ere John could speak,
"He's but a baby, too" said I,
And kissed him as we hurried by.
Pale, patient Robbie's angel face
Still in his sleep bore suffering's trace.
"No, for a thousand crowns, not him!"
We whispered, while our eyes were dim.
Poor Dick! bad Dick! our wayward son,
Turbulent, reckless, idle one —
Could he be spared? Nay; He who gave
Bids us befriend him to his grave;
"Only a mother's heart can be
Patient enough for such as he;
And so," said John, "I would not dare
To send him from her bedside prayer."
Then stole we softly up above
And knelt by Mary, child of love.
"Perhaps for her 'twould better be,"
I said to John. Quite silently
He lifted up a curl astray
Across her cheek in wilful way,
And shook his head: "Nay, love; not thee" —
The while my heart beat audibly.
Only one more, our eldest lad,
Trusty and truthful, good and glad —
So like his father. "No, John, no —
I cannot, will not, let him go."
And so we wrote, in courteous way,
We could not give one child away;

(continued overleaf)

And afterward toil lighter seemed,
Thinking of that of which we dreamed,
Happy in truth that not one face
We missed from its accustomed place;
Thankful to work for all the seven,
Trusting the rest to One in heaven.

ETHELINDA BEERS

Lean Hard

Child of My love, lean hard,
And let Me feel the pressure of thy care.
I know thy burden, child, I shaped it,
Poised it in Mine own hand; made no proportion
Between its weight and thine unaided strength;
For even as I laid it on, I said,
"I shall be near and while she leans on Me,
This burden shall be Mine, not hers:
So shall I keep My child
Within th' encircling arms of My own Love."

Here lay it down, nor fear
To impose it on a shoulder which upholds
The government of worlds. Yet closer come!
Thou art not near enough. I would embrace thy care.
Thou lovest Me! I know it. Doubt not then,
But, loving Me, *lean hard!*

CHARLOTTE BICKERSTETH WARD

This poem, written around 1870, was inspired by an incident which occurred on a
visit to Switzerland. The author saw two people walking on a steep hill road, one
an elderly woman and the other a young girl. The girl was heard to say to her com-
panion "Lean on me — lean hard".

Prayer for a Very New Angel

God, God be lenient . . . her first night there.
The crib she slept in was so near my bed;
Her blue-and-white wool blanket was so soft,
Her pillow hollowed so to fit her head.

Teach me that she'll not want
Small rooms or me,
When she has You and Heaven's immensity.

I always left a light out in the hall,
I hoped to make her fearless in the dark;
And yet, she was so small — one little light
Not in the room, it scarcely mattered. Hark!

No, no; she seldom cried!
God, not too far
For her to see, this first night, light a star!

And in the morning, when she first woke up,
I always kissed her on her left cheek where
The dimple was. And oh, I wet the brush.
It made it easier to curl her hair.

Just, just tomorrow morning,
God, I pray,
When she wakes up, do things for her my way!

VIOLET ALLEYN STOREY

The Roman Centurion's Song

(Roman occupation of Britain, A.D. 300)

Legate, I had the news last night — my cohort ordered home
By ship to Portus Itius and thence by road to Rome.
I've marched the companies aboard, the arms are
    stowed below:
Now let another take my sword. Command me not to go!

I've served in Britain forty years, from Vectis to the Wall.
I have none other home than this, nor any life at all.
Last night I did not understand, but, now the hour draws near
That calls me to my native land, I feel that land is here.

Here where men say my name was made, here where my
    work was done;
Here where my dearest dead are laid — my wife — my
    wife and son;
Here where time, custom, grief and toil, age, memory,
    service, love,
Have rooted me in British soil. Ah, how can I remove?

For me this land, that sea, these airs, those folk and fields suffice.
What purple Southern pomp can match our changeful
    Northern skies,
Black with December snows unshed or pearled with
    August haze —
The clanging arch of steel-grey March, or June's long-
    lighted days?

You'll follow widening Rhodanus till vine and olive lean
Aslant before the sunny breeze that sweeps Nemausus clean
To Arelate's triple gate; but let me linger on,
Here where our stiff-necked British oaks confront
    Euroclydon!

You'll take the old Aurelian Road through shore-
    descending pines
Where, blue as any peacock's neck, the Tyrrhene Ocean shines.
You'll go where laurel crowns are won, but — will you
    e'er forget
The scent of hawthorn in the sun, or bracken in the wet?

Let me work here for Britain's sake — at any task you will —
A marsh to drain, a road to make or native troops to drill.
Some Western camp (I know the Pict) or granite Border keep,
Mid seas of heather derelict, where our old messmates sleep.

Legate, I come to you in tears — My cohort ordered home!
I've served in Britain forty years. What should I do in Rome?
Here is my heart, my soul, my mind — the only life I know.
I cannot leave it all behind. Command me not to go!

RUDYARD KIPLING

Norman and Saxon

"My son" said the Norman Baron, "I am dying, and you will be heir
To all the broad acres in England that William gave me for my share
When we conquered the Saxon at Hastings, and a nice little
    handful it is.
But before you go over to rule it I want you to understand this:—

"The Saxon is not like us Normans. His manners are not so polite.
But he never means anything serious till he talks about justice
    and right.
When he stands like an ox in the furrow with his sullen set eyes on
    your own,
And grumbles, 'This isn't fair dealing,' my son, leave the Saxon alone.

"You can horsewhip your Gascony archers, or torture your
   Picardy spears;
But don't try that game on the Saxon; you'll have the whole brood
   round your ears.
From the richest old Thane in the county to the poorest chained
   serf in the field,
They'll be at you and on you like hornets, and, if you are wise, you
   will yield.

"But first you must master their language, their dialect, proverbs
   and songs.
Don't trust any clerk to interpret when they come with the tale of
   their wrongs.
Let them know that you know what they're saying; let them feel that
   you know what to say.
Yes, even when you want to go hunting, hear 'em out if it takes you
   all day.

"They'll drink every hour of the daylight and poach every hour of
   the dark.
It's the sport not the rabbits they're after (we've plenty of game in
   the park).
Don't hang them or cut off their fingers. That's wasteful as well as
   unkind,
For a hard-bitten South-country poacher makes the best man-at-arms
   you can find.

"Appear with your wife and the children at their weddings and
   funerals and feasts.
Be polite but not friendly to Bishops; be good to all poor
   parish priests.
Say 'we,' 'us' and 'ours' when you're talking, instead of 'you fellows'
   and 'I'.
Don't ride over seeds; keep your temper; and *never you tell 'em a lie!*"

                                                    RUDYARD KIPLING

Autumn Leaves

"Come little leaves", said the wind one day,
"Come o'er the meadows with me and play
Put on your dresses of red and gold
Summer is gone and the days grow cold."

Soon as the leaves heard the wind's loud call
Down they came tumbling one and all
Over the brown fields they danced and flew
Singing the soft little songs they knew.

"Cricket goodbye, we've been friends so long,
Little brook sing us your farewell song,
Say you are sorry to see us go
Ah, you will miss us right well we know.

"Dear little lambs in your fleecy fold,
Mother will keep you from harm and cold,
Fondly we've watched you in vale and glade
Pray will you dream of our loving shade?"

Dancing and whirling the little leaves went,
Winter had called them and they were content.
Soon, fast asleep in their earthly beds
The snow laid a coverlet over their heads.

GEORGE COOPER

Grandmother's old Armchair

My grandmother, she, at the age of eighty-three,
  One day in May was taken ill and died;
And after she was dead the will of course was read
  By a lawyer as we all stood side by side.
To my brother, it was found, she had left a hundred pound,
  The same unto my sister, I declare;
But when it came to me the lawyer said, "I see
  She has left to you her old armchair."

CHORUS:

  How they tittered, how they chaffed,
  How my brother and sister laughed,
  When they heard the lawyer declare
  Granny'd only left to me her old armchair.

I thought it hardly fair, still I said I did not care,
  And in the evening took the chair away,
My brother at me laughed, the lawyer at me chaffed,
  And said, "It will come useful, John, some day
When you settle down in life,
Find some girl to be your wife,
  You'll find it very handy, I declare;
On a cold and frosty night,
When the fire is burning bright,
  You can sit in your old armchair."

What the lawyer said was true,
For in a year or two,
  Strange to say, I settled down in married life.
I first a girl did court and then the ring I bought,
  Took her to the church, and then she was my wife.
Now the dear girl and me
Are happy as can be,
  And when my work is over, I declare,
I ne'er abroad would roam,
But each night I'd stay at home,
  And be seated in my old armchair.

(continued overleaf)

One night the chair fell down.
When I picked it up I found
   The seat had fallen out upon the floor,
And there before my eyes
I saw to my surprise,
   A lot of notes, ten thousand pounds or more.
When my brother heard of this,
The poor fellow, I confess,
   Went nearly wild with rage and tore his hair.
But I only laughed at him,
And I said unto him: "Jim,
   Don't you wish you had the old armchair?"

No more they tittered, no more they chaffed,
No more my brother and my sister laughed,
When they heard the lawyer declare
Granny'd only left to me her old armchair.

ANON

138

The Old Arm-Chair

I love it! I love it! And who shall dare
To chide me for loving that old arm-chair?
I've treasured it long as a sainted prize;
I've bedewed it with tears, and embalmed it with sighs.
'Tis bound by a thousand bands to my heart;
Not a tie will break, not a link will start.
Would ye learn the spell? — a mother sat there;
And a sacred thing is that old arm-chair.

In childhood's hour I lingered near
The hallowed seat with list'ning ear;
And gentle words that mother would give,
To fit me to die, and teach me to live.
She told me shame would never betide
With truth for my creed, and God for my guide;
She taught me to lisp my earliest prayer,
As I knelt beside that old arm-chair.

I sat and watched her many a day,
When her eyes grew dim, and her locks were grey;
And I almost worshipped her when she smiled,
And turned from her Bible to bless her child.
Years rolled on; but the last one sped —
My idol was shattered; my earth-star fled.
I learnt how much the heart can bear,
When I saw her die in the old arm-chair.

'Tis past! 'tis past! But I gaze on it now
With quivering breath and sobbing brow:
'Twas there she nursed me; 'twas there she died:
And memory flows with lava tide.
Say it is folly, and deem me weak,
While the scalding drops start down my cheek;
But I love it! I love it! and cannot tear
My soul from a mother's old arm-chair.

ELIZA COOK.

The Perfect Guest

She answered by return of post
The invitation of her host.
She caught the train she said she would
And changed at junctions as she should.
She brought a light and smallish box
And keys belonging to the locks.
Food, strange and rare, she did not beg,
But ate the homely scrambled egg.
When offered lukewarm tea she drank it.
She did not crave an extra blanket,
Nor extra pillows for her head:
She seemed to like the spare-room bed.
She never came downstairs till ten,
She brought her own self-filling pen,
Nor once by look or word of blame
Exposed her host to open shame.
She left no little things behind,
Excepting... loving thoughts and kind.

ROSE HENNIKER HEATON

The Perfect Pest

She merely sent a wire to say
That she was coming down to stay.
She brought a maid of minxsome look
Who promptly quarrelled with the cook.
She smoked, and dropped with ruthless hand
Hot ashes on the Steinway grand.
She strode across the parquet floors
With hobnailed boots from out of doors.
She said the water wasn't hot,
And Jane gave notice on the spot.
She snubbed the wealthy dull relations

From whom my wife had expectations.
She kept her bell in constant peals,
She never was in time for meals.
And when at last with joyful heart
We thrust her in the luggage cart,
In half an hour she came again,
And said . . . "My dear, I've missed the train!"

ADRIAN PORTER

Mother was a Lady

Two drummers sat at dinner, in a grand hotel one day,
While dining they were chatting in a jolly sort of way,
And when a pretty waitress brought them a tray of food,
They spoke to her familiarly in a manner rather rude;
At first she did not notice them or make the least reply,
But one remark was passed that brought teardrops to her eye,
And facing her tormentor, with cheeks now burning red,
She looked a perfect picture as appealingly she said,

"My mother was a lady like yours you will allow,
And you may have a sister, who needs protection now.
I've come to this great city
To find a brother dear.
And you wouldn't dare insult me, Sir,
If only Jack were here."

It's true one touch of nature, it makes the whole world kin,
And every word she uttered seemed to touch their hearts within,
They sat there stunned and silent, until one cried in shame,
"Forgive me Miss! I meant no harm, pray tell me what's
    your name."

(continued overleaf)

She told him and he cried again, "I know your brother too,
Why we've been friends for many years and he often
    speaks of you,
He'll be so glad to see you, and if you'll only wed,
I'll take you to him as my wife, for I loved you since you said."

"My mother was a lady like yours you will allow,
And you may have a sister, who needs protection now.
I've come to this great city
To find a brother dear.
And you wouldn't dare insult me, Sir,
If only Jack were here."

EDWARD B. MARKS

Alone on the Raft

Alone on the raft in the twilight,
Afloat on the mighty deep,
A poor sailor-lad was lying
On the drifting planks, asleep;
For his vessel was wrecked in a tempest
That swept all the crew to rest,
All but the poor little sailor boy
Alone on the ocean's breast.

The cold night wind soon awoke him
From his brief and restless sleep
And he gazed with a look, oh! so eager
O'er the waves of the silent deep.
There was no dim light in the distance,
No gleam of a passing sail,
And the sailor boy's heart grew heavy and sad
As his last hope seemed to fail.

He knelt down at last in the darkness
And cried, as he looked above,
"O Father on high, have mercy,
And save me in thy love!"
Then, weary and faint with hunger,
He fell like a log on the raft;
While, silent and low, the wind did blow,
Softly rocking the little craft.

When life came back to him slowly
There were kind faces clustered round
On the deck of a gallant vessel
So swiftly homeward bound;
They had spied him at early morning
Afloat on the drifting raft,
And they picked up the poor little ocean waif,
And brought him on board their craft;

And a cheer rang out from the seamen
As he stood right up by the mast,
He could scarce speak for joy, the poor sailor boy,
They had saved from the sea at last!

HENRY VAUGHAN

143